CHOSEN

A study on the book of Ephesians

By
KRISTIN SCHMUCKER

STUDY CONTRIBUTORS

Designer:
MICHELE YATES

Editor:
MELISSA DENNIS

Contributing Author:
SARAH MORRISON

www.thedailygraceco.com

Unless otherwise noted all Scripture has been taken from the Christian Standard Bible®, Copyright © 2017 by Holman Bible Publishers. Used by permission. Christian Standard Bible® and CSB® are federally registered trademarks of Holman Bible Publishers.

Designed in the United States of America and printed in China.

Study Suggestions

Thank you for choosing this study to help you dig into God's Word. We are so passionate about women getting into Scripture, and we are praying that this study will be a tool to help you do that. Here are a few tips to help you get the most from this study:

- Before you begin, take time to look into the context of the book. Find out who wrote it and learn about the cultural climate it was written in, as well as where it fits on the biblical timeline. Then take time to read through the entire book of the Bible we are studying if you are able. This will help you to get the big picture of the book and will aid in comprehension, interpretation, and application.

- Start your study time with prayer. Ask God to help you understand what you are reading and allow it to transform you (Psalm 119:18).

- Look into the context of the book as well as the specific passage.

- Before reading what is written in the study, read the assigned passage! Repetitive reading is one of the best ways to study God's Word. Read it several times, if you are able, before going on to the study. Read in several translations if you find it helpful.

- As you read the text, mark down observations and questions. Write down things that stand out to you, things that you notice, or things that you don't understand. Look up important words in a dictionary or interlinear Bible.

- Look for things like verbs, commands, and references to God. Notice key terms and themes throughout the passage.

- After you have worked through the text, read what is written in the study. Take time to look up any cross-references mentioned as you study.

• Then work through the questions provided in the book. Read and answer them prayerfully.

• Paraphrase or summarize the passage, or even just one verse from the passage. Putting it into your own words helps you to slow down and think through every word.

• Focus your heart on the character of God that you have seen in this passage. What do you learn about God from the passage you have studied? Adore Him and praise Him for who He is.

• Think and pray through application and how this passage should change you. Get specific with yourself. Resist the urge to apply the passage to others. Do you have sin to confess? How should this passage impact your attitude toward people or circumstances? Does the passage command you to do something? Do you need to trust Him for something in your life? How does the truth of the gospel impact your everyday life?

• We recommend you have a Bible, pen, highlighters, and journal as you work through this study. We recommend that ball point pens instead of gel pens be used in the study book to prevent smearing. Here are several other optional resources that you may find helpful as you study:

• www.blueletterbible.org This free website is a great resource for digging deeper. You can find translation comparison, an interlinear option to look at words in the original languages, Bible dictionaries, and even commentary.

• A Dictionary. If looking up words in the Hebrew and Greek feels intimidating, look up words in English. Often times we assume we know the meaning of a word, but looking it up and seeing its definition can help us understand a passage better.

• A double-spaced copy of the text. You can use a website like www.biblegateway.com to copy the text of a passage and print out a double-spaced copy to be able to mark on easily. Circle, underline, highlight, draw arrows, and mark in any way you would like to help you dig deeper and work through a passage.

PAUL'S RELATIONSHIP WITH THE EPHESIANS

AD 52
ACTS 18:18-21

Paul leaves Corinth to sail to Ephesus and reasons with the Jews in an Ephesian Synagogue. The Jews there asked him to stay longer, but he declined and said, "I will return to you if God wills."

AD 56
ACTS 19:21

Paul leaves Ephesus to go to Jerusalem

AD 60
ACTS 28:16

Paul writes letter to the Ephesians while imprisoned under house arrest in Rome.

CIRCA AD 67-68
Paul's Death

AD 54
ACTS 19:1-7

Paul finds disciples of John the Baptist in Ephesus. He teaches them about the Holy Spirit, and they are converted, and baptized.

ACTS 19:8-12

Paul stays in Ephesus, speaking in the synagogue for three months, making proclamations about God. The name of God becomes revered in the region and many denounce their pagan practices because of it (19:18-20).

AD 57
ACTS 20:17-38

Paul returns to Ephesus to say goodbye to the Ephesian Elders, knowing that he will never see them again.

AD 62
1 TIM 1:3

Paul instructs Timothy to remain in Ephesus, continuing to the work that had begun

Timeline: AD 50 — AD 55 — AD 60 — AD 65 — AD 70

INTRODUCTION
to Ephesians

WEEK ONE
♦ ♦ ♦
DAY ONE

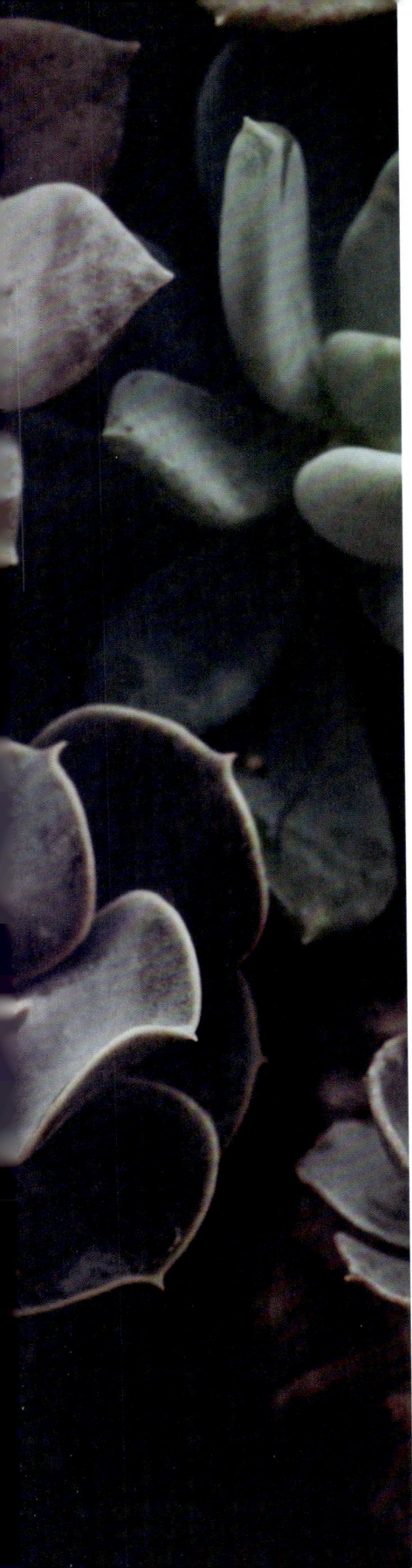

Read the Entire Book of Ephesians

◆ ◆ ◆

Who are we? How should we live? These are the questions of the book of Ephesians. In the first half of the book, Paul takes time to carefully show us our identity and who we are in Christ. "In him" and varieties of this phrase are some of the most important phrases through all of the book of Ephesians. These small words reveal to us that through salvation we have been united with Christ. He is in us and we are in Him, and this changes how we view everything in the world. We look at ourselves as believers who are in Christ. His identity changes our identity. And then we look at our practical everyday lives in light of this union with Christ. We live differently because we are in Him.

The book of Ephesians holds some of the most well-known verses and passages of Scripture, but it is my prayer that as we slowly study this short book and see it as one glorious whole that we will be left in awe of our Savior, comforted by our position in Him, and compelled to live lives that seek to bring glory to Him.

INTRODUCTION
Continued

WEEK ONE
♦♦♦
DAY TWO

Take time today to read through the entire book of Ephesians! If possible try to do it in one sitting. Make note below of every time a phrase like "in him," or "in Christ" appears.

Today take time to read through the entire book of Ephesians at least one more time before we dig into each verse.

◆ ◆ ◆

What key words or phrases stand out to you in the book of Ephesians?

What verse stands out to you after reading the entire book?

Are there any questions that you have after reading the book?

Take a moment to write out a prayer asking God to help you know Him more through the study of Ephesians.

GRACE and PEACE

WEEK ONE
♦ ♦ ♦
DAY THREE

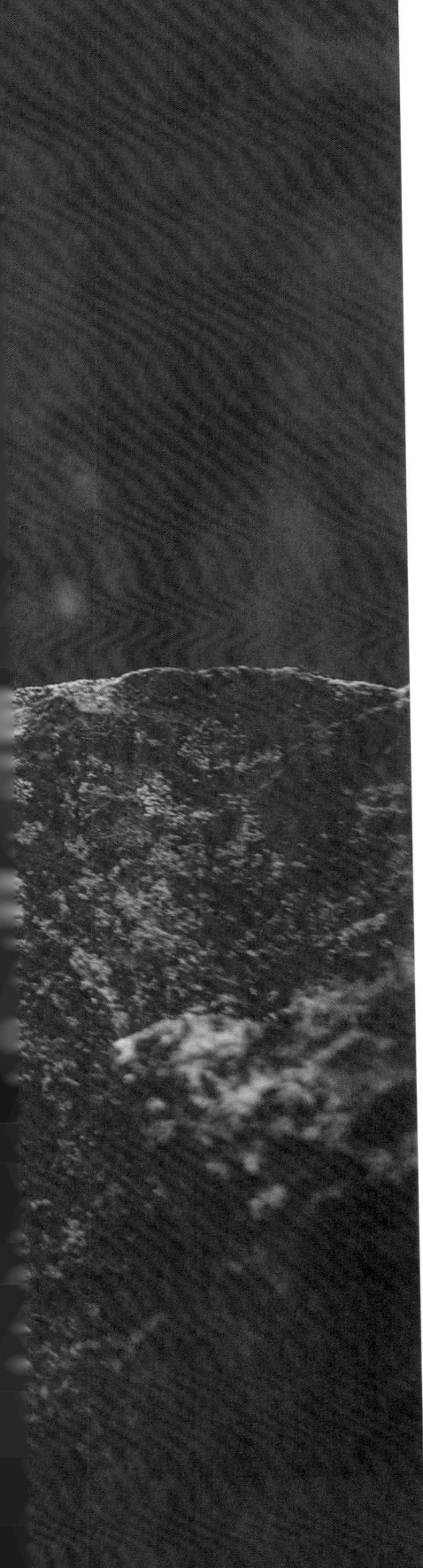

Ephesians 1:1-2

♦ ♦ ♦

Ephesians tells us who we are and how we should live. It tells us our identity in Christ, and it tells us God's will for our lives. It tells us that we are in Him because of salvation and that we should also live in Him.

The book of Ephesians was written by the apostle Paul. Paul was an enemy of God and a persecutor of Christians (Acts 9:1-2). Born a Jew, he was now an apostle of Jesus to the Gentiles (Romans 11:13). Paul had been called and set apart before he was born (Galatians 1:15-16) so that he could preach the gospel. Now, "by the will of God," he would bring a message of grace and peace to the Ephesians and to us today. These words, likely written from prison, were written from a man who clearly loved the church he was writing to. After spending over three years there, it was the longest place that Paul ever ministered. Paul reminds us that God changes people, and He can use anyone — even us. May we never get stuck in the thinking that "this is just the way I am," because this mindset negates the sovereign power of our God to change any person. Just as Paul had a purpose to fulfill, we have been given a part in God's story as well. God has placed you exactly where you are, and you can serve Him right here. Paul very likely wrote this letter from prison, and yet even there, he served the Lord. May we serve God right where He has us with everything that we are. May we never think that we need a different position or a different situation to be faithful to what He has called us to do. *It is no accident that you are where you are.*

The letter is written to the saints at Ephesus. The word "saints" here literally means "holy," and it is a reminder again of the theme of the book, that we have been made holy in Him and are now called to live holy lives. The city of Ephesus was a busy first century port city, similar to our major metropolitan cities. It was also a seedbed of paganism, materialism, idolatry, immorality, and the occult. The church was a shining light in a dark place. Ephesus was home to the temple of Diana, and much unrest came as Christianity began to spread and put idol-makers out of business. The church was spreading the gospel, and the gospel was disrupting the culture. These words were written to the faithful, or the ones that had believed in God. These saints and faithful believers in Ephesus are identified as being in Christ, a phrase that appears 36 times in the book of Ephesians. The greeting of the book is a greeting of grace and peace which are themes that will be seen over and over in the book of Ephesians.

It is in Christ alone that we find grace and peace. We are His chosen people, set apart to love and serve Him, and it is in Him that we find everything that we need because He is our everything.

◆ ◆ ◆

Paul was called to be an apostle by the will of God. He has called us as well and placed us right where He wants us to be. What role does God have you in right now?

How can you serve God right where you are?

How were the Christians of Ephesus described in Ephesians 1:1? What words do you want to be used by others to describe you?

CHOSEN

WEEK ONE
• • •
DAY FOUR

Ephesians 1:3-6

◆ ◆ ◆

As Paul moved from the introduction of the book to the heart of the book, we find one complex and beautiful sentence from verses 3-14. It is 202 words in the original Greek. These words of praise to our God have been likened to many things throughout the centuries. In my mind, I see them as a symphony of praise to our Creator. Beginning with just one instrument, it slowly builds adding instrument after instrument as the crescendo of praise builds and builds. This is what Paul is doing in this massive sentence as he describes who our God is and what He has done. This passage does deal with topics that are hard for us to fully understand, but above all, it is a declaration of praise to a God who is so much greater than our understanding. We bless Him because "in Christ," He has blessed us. We see in these verses the "already, but not yet" of our faith. Positionally in Christ, we already have every spiritual blessing, and practically we are constantly growing closer to our Redeemer and to the day when we will see in full every spiritual blessing. Our redemption has taken place at the cross and we await with expectation the restoration that is to come.

This passage points to all three persons of the trinity. We see God the Father choosing to bless us in the Son and sealing us with the Holy Spirit. These verses clearly and beautifully set forth the truth that we were chosen and predestined before the foundation of the world. In the Greek, these words are in the aorist tense, which means that they are definite. *This is a done deal.* We find ourselves trying to understand how to justify the tension of God's sovereign choice and man's free will, but we do not need to force our human understanding on this divine truth. As we read and try to understand all of His ways, we must also remember that He is God and we are not. The mystery and tension of this should leave us in awe of a God whose ways are higher than our ways and propel us to worship just as Paul was when He wrote these words. He has chosen us to be holy and blameless, which is only possible because we are in Jesus Christ. He has predestined us for adoption. We are made sons and daughters of God through what Jesus has done. And all of this truth was part of His great plan and will for us, and it is all made possible *in Christ*. There is nothing we could do to earn this on our own — He has lavished His grace freely upon us. Verse 6 clearly tells us the reason for it all. We are His to praise His glorious grace. We have been saved by grace through faith to bring glory to our God. May we stand in awe of the truth of who our God is and all that He has done for us. He has chosen us to be His own.

> "There is nothing we could do to earn this on our own—He has lavished His grace freely upon us."

How is knowing that you have been chosen by God comforting to you? Romans 12:1-2 remind us that we are transformed by the renewing of our minds. Thinking the way God thinks changes us! How can the knowledge of who you are in Christ change the way you think about yourself and your life?

Positionally we already have been given every spiritual blessing in Christ, and yet day by day we are growing to be more like Him. How can you practically seek to grow closer to God this week?

These verses are words of worship from Paul who was left in awe of who God is and all that He has done. Take a few moments to write out your own words of worship thanking God for who He is and what He has done for you.

Ephesians 1:7-10

❖ ❖ ❖

Today's verses begin with the beautiful truth that we have redemption. We have been delivered from our bondage to sin by our Savior. In this passage we see the entire Trinity, and today we see the ministry of the Son in our salvation. It is in Him that we have redemption. We do not just hope for redemption, we have it. *It is finished*. This gives great assurance for all who have put faith in His saving grace. We do not hope that we will be saved, but we have full assurance. We *know* that we have eternal life (1 John 5:13). It is through the blood of our Savior that we have redemption and forgiveness. The concept of redemption means that He has paid the price for us. He has done what we could not do. Because of Jesus, our lives as His children will never be the same. He has set us free from the sin that enslaved us and then adopted us as His own children (Galatians 4:3-7). Forgiveness means "carried away," and He has carried away our sins as far as the east is from the west (Psalm 103:12). This was pictured in the Old Testament during the Day of Atonement. The priest would sacrifice a goat and then take a second goat and confess the sins of the people over it. The goat would then be released — never to be seen again.

Jesus is our scape goat. In the same way, Jesus was sacrificed for us, and then He carried our sin away — never to be seen again.

In salvation we gain the righteousness of God in exchange for the sin that had once separated us from our Savior (2 Corinthians 5:21). It is only through His unspeakable and immeasurable grace that this great salvation has been made possible. And now we see that His plan from the beginning has been to unite all things to Himself. Again, we see the "already and not yet" of our faith. We have *already* been justified and united with Christ, and now we await the day that has *not yet* occurred, when all of creation will be restored and sin will be erased (Revelation 21:4). In these verses that continue this enormous sentence of praise, we see Paul's eternal perspective, and it reminds us that we should have the same perspective. We should set our minds on things above as Paul tells us in Colossians 3:2. We should remember and praise Him for what He has done in eternity past and also gaze ahead at eternity future, praising Him for what He will do. It has been said by many theologians that "theology leads to doxology," and it is so true. When we see just a glimpse of who our God is, we will not be able to keep from praising Him as we find ourselves overwhelmed with His goodness.

> "He has set us free from the sin that enslaved us and then adopted us as His own children"

If you have trusted His grace, you have been redeemed. You are no longer a slave to sin but are now a child of God. What would your life be like without redemption?

In Christ, we also find forgiveness. Our sins have been paid for, carried away, and forgiven. How should the knowledge of forgiveness change the way we live each day, as well as how we deal with sin in our lives as believers.

How does theology (what we believe about God) lead to doxology (praise to God)?

For he chose us in him, before the foundation of the world, to be holy and blameless in love before him.

• • •

Ephesians 1:4

WEEKLY REFLECTION

Read Ephesians 1:1-10

- Paraphrase the passage from this week.

- What did you observe from this week's text about God and His character?

- What does the passage teach about the condition of mankind and about yourself?

Week One

- How does this passage point to the gospel?

- How should you respond to this passage? What is the personal application?

- What specific action steps can you take this week to apply the passage?

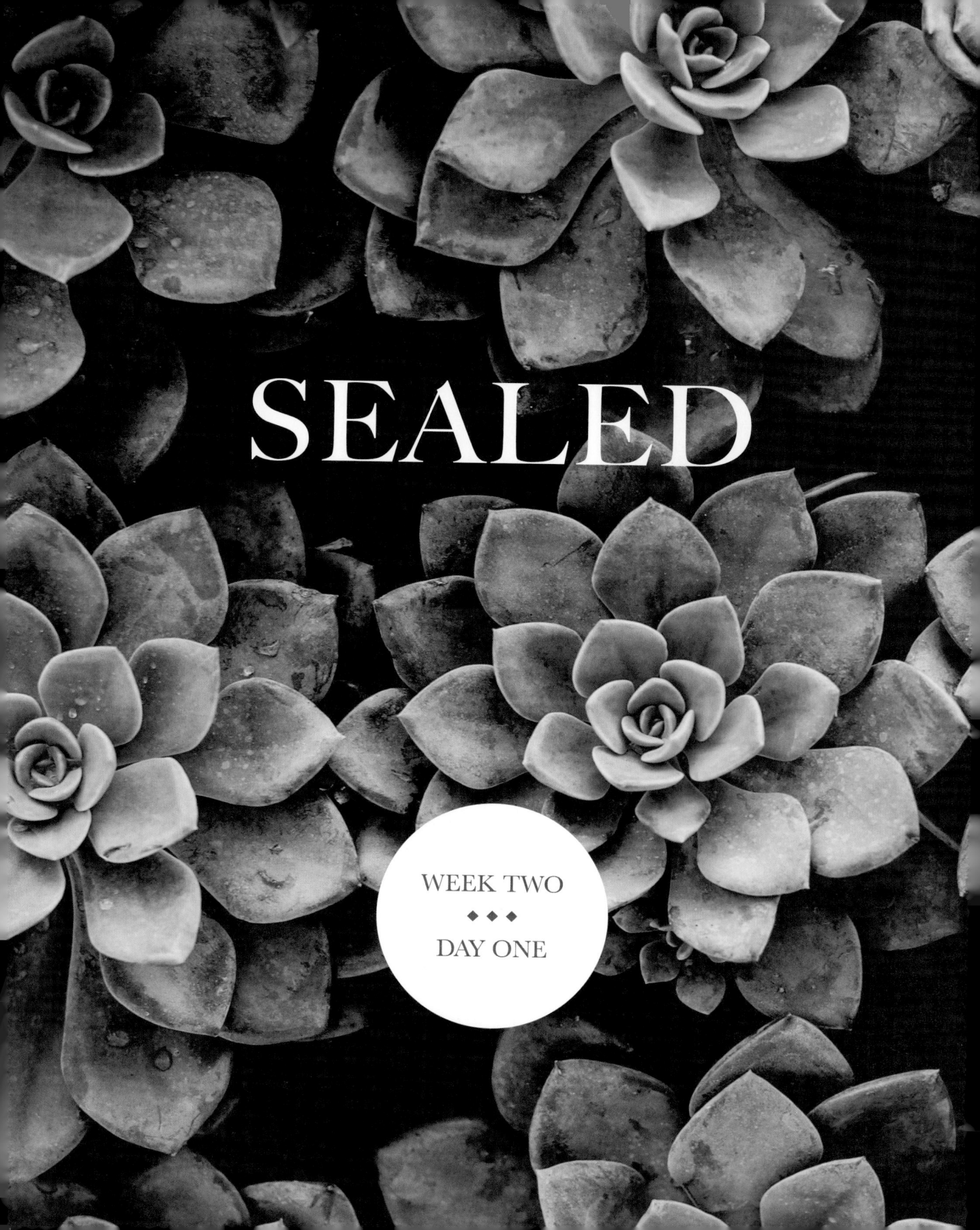

Ephesians 1:11-14

◆ ◆ ◆

In this passage, Paul reminds the Ephesian church that both Jews and Gentiles are saved by His grace to the praise of His glory. Galatians 3:28-29 reminds us that we are one in Christ Jesus. The inheritance in verse 11 may refer to the truth that we are God's inheritance as was illustrated throughout the Old Testament (Deuteronomy 4:20, Psalm 33:12, 135:4), or it may refer to the truth that in Christ we receive an inheritance (Colossians 1:12). Both truths are clearly presented in Scripture, and scholars fall on both sides. Either way, these verses make it clear that both Jews and Gentiles take part in this great salvation. The Jews are referred to as the first to hope in Christ, and the Gentiles are referred to as "you also." God has given us a new identity in Himself. We are no longer Jew or Gentile, slave or free, male or female — in Jesus we are all *one*. We are no longer defined by what the world tells us we are. We are who *He* says we are. We are chosen, loved, and redeemed. *We are His*.

Over and over in this chapter, we are reminded that God does all things according to the purpose of His sovereign will, and yet we also see here that our response in faith is a part of this mystery of God's sovereignty. But it is all for the praise of His glory. Both Jews and Gentiles believe because of His sovereign plan, and for the purpose of bringing Him glory.

We have been sealed with the Holy Spirit. The seal mentioned here is like the animals that were branded by their masters; it was a symbol of ownership. Our seal shows that we are owned by our Savior, the One who paid the price to redeem us. In verse 14, we see that the Holy Spirit is the guarantee, or the down payment, of our inheritance. The Holy Spirit within us is just a taste of all that God has for His children. The Spirit is the "already" of the "already and not yet" of our faith. With the Spirit inside us, we have a sweet glimpse of what the future holds for us as God's people. We have been chosen by God the Father, redeemed by Jesus the Son, and sealed by the Holy Spirit. And it is all to the praise of His glory. John Stott said, "Thus everything we have and are in Christ both comes from God and returns to God. It begins in His will and ends in His glory. For this is where everything begins and ends." We have been created for His glory. We have been chosen for His glory. We have been redeemed for His glory. We now live for His glory. *We are His for His glory.*

> **"The Holy Spirit within us is just a taste of all that God has for His children."**

What are the lies that the world tries to tell you about who you are/your identity?
Who does God say that you are?

Throughout the book of Ephesians, we see the phrase "in Him" repeated.
What does it mean to be in Him?

How should the truth that we are "in Him" change the way we live?

In what ways is the Holy Spirit inside us a glimpse of what eternity will be like with God?

THAT I MAY
Know Him

WEEK TWO

❖❖❖

DAY TWO

Ephesians 1:15-23

◆ ◆ ◆

The beginning of Ephesians 1 was praise to our God for who He is and what He has done. Paul continues His praise in the form of a prayer in the next section. The prayer begins with Paul giving thanks to God for this church and for the grace of God displayed in their lives. We are often quick to be critical of other believers, but Paul reminds us to thank God for the saints. We then see what Paul prayed for this church. These words that Paul prays for these churches in Asia are so applicable for us as well. Paul prays for them to have understanding and knowledge. He wants the believers to know the Lord. This prayer is for God to open the eyes of their hearts so that they could know Him. We see similar wording in other passages such as Psalm 119:18, where the psalmist prays for his eyes to be opened to the truths of God's Word, and also in Philippians 3:10 in a prayer for us to know Him and the power of His resurrection. May this be our prayer as well, that we would know Him and know His power in our own lives. Paul speaks of this power here as well, and it will be the subject of the remainder of the chapter.

God's power for us as believers is described

as "immeasurable greatness." The Greek word for power here is *dynamis* — it is a miracle working power, and the word from which we get our English word "dynamite." This power is in us as believers (Romans 8:11). This is the power that raised Jesus from the dead. It is the power that has Him sitting at the right hand of the Father, and it is the power by which He rules the church. This is the power by which He will one day bring restoration and make all that is wrong in the world right again. *And this power is in us*. Strong enough to handle anything that we may face in this life, and God is willing to give us this because we are His chosen people. This glorious chapter gives us a full view of what God has done for us through Jesus. He has called us from the beginning. He has made us an inheritance in the end. And in the present, He has given us His mighty power. The more we see and learn of Him, the more our hearts yearn to know more.

> "May this be our prayer as well, that we would know Him and know His power in our own lives."

Write out a prayer of praise to the Lord.

*List some ways that you are thankful for other believers.
Who is someone that has encouraged you to grow closer to the Lord?*

How do we grow in our knowledge of God and His power?

Ephesians 2:1-6

✦ ✦ ✦

A glimpse of our condition before we met Jesus gives us a renewed gratitude for what God has done for us. We will see in this passage a long and painful look at the state of humanity without the Savior, and a reminder that this was once us as well. The language Paul uses feels hopeless. We were *dead* in our trespasses and sins.

We were spiritually dead with no hope in sight, and no power to bring ourselves back to life. A distinction is made here between our trespasses and sin, and the Greek words indicate the fullness of our fallen condition. Trespasses (*paraptoma*) refers to us willfully crossing boundary lines. Sins (*hamartia*) means missing the mark or not living up to God's standard of righteousness and perfection. The careful wording of the passage shows us that we have both passively and actively fallen short of God's righteousness. Passively because we are fallen people unable to be perfect, and actively because we choose each day our own way instead of His way. We lived in that state of sin before Christ. We were slaves to sin, constantly trying to satisfy our souls with temporary pleasure. Like running on a treadmill, we were expelling all of our energy, but not getting anywhere. *We needed regeneration. We needed resurrection.* We were oppressed from the world outside and our own sinful selves inside. Then come two words that change everything — "But God." We were dead in our sins, *but God* made us alive. We were willfully disobedient, *but God* showed mercy to us. We were running from Him, *but God* was running to us. He loved us while we were dead in our sins and far from Him. He took what was dead and made us alive. Like the valley of dry bones in Ezekiel 37, we were completely dead and completely hopeless, but our God brings dead things to life (Ezekiel 37:1-14, Romans 4:17). He changed everything. Gloria Furman says, "Whereas before, we were dead in our sin, when we are co-crucified with Christ, we become dead to our sin." We don't just need to try to change the things we do; we need to let Christ change who we are.

Those that have placed their faith in Him have been saved and made alive. Those two little words, "but God," tell our story and the story of every believer. John Stott says, "Indeed the major emphasis of this whole paragraph is that what prompted God to act on our behalf was not something in us (some supposed merit) but something in himself (his own unmerited favour)." He tells us His purpose in it all. He has shown His grace and mercy and made us heirs with Christ, and He will keep showing His grace to us for all of eternity. May we praise Him for those two little words "But God," that changed everything for us, and for the matchless grace poured out on all who believe.

> "We were running from Him, but God was running to us."

Our passage today tells us about our state before Jesus. How does the knowledge of our fallen condition make us grateful for what God has done for us?

Take time to meditate on those glorious words, "But God." Take time to think through this sentence and rewrite it as a way of remembering what God has done for you.

I was _____ but God, _____.

Romans 2:4 tells us that it is God's kindness that leads us to repentance. This passage reminds us of His incredible kindness and grace in drawing us to Himself. Because of how God has so kindly dealt with you, how can you extend grace to others?

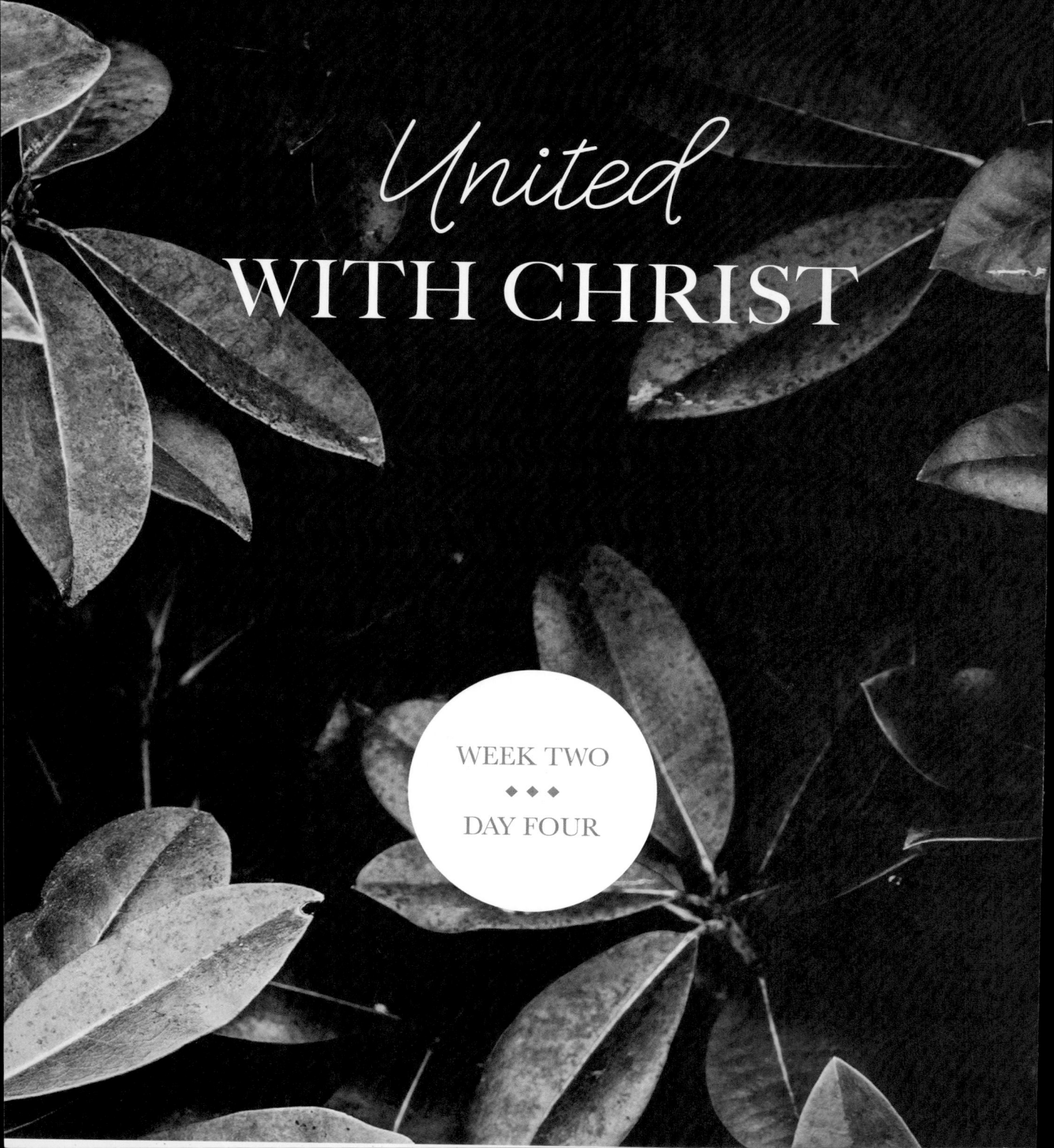

United
WITH CHRIST

WEEK TWO
♦ ♦ ♦
DAY FOUR

Ephesians 2:6-7

♦ ♦ ♦

We have been united with Christ because of His mercy and love. Yesterday we looked at our desperate condition and the two small words that change everything. When we were destitute and hopeless, Jesus came to us. When we were dead in our sins with no power to resurrect ourselves, Jesus breathed life into our lifeless bodies.

Just as Jesus was resurrected from the tomb, our dead hearts have been raised from the grave of our sin. Baptism shows us the beautiful picture of what happens in conversion as we are buried in the likeness of His death and raised to walk in newness of life. The moment of our salvation has eternal results. And it is all because of His mercy and love toward us through Jesus.

We have been crucified with Christ and our sin has been put to death (Romans 6:5-11, Galatians 2:20). Here Paul tells us that we have been made alive with Christ and raised, or ascended, with Him. Just as we were crucified with Him, we are also raised with Him. But Paul goes one glorious step further. Not only have we been crucified, buried, raised, ascended, but we have also been seated with

Him in the heavenly places. At first thought this may seem silly to us. How can I be raised to heaven while I sit here in my home with a coffee cup in hand? Paul is declaring the glory of our union with Christ that in salvation not only is Christ in us, but we are in Him. As a child of God we are inseparable from Jesus. So though we are here on this earth, we are united to the One that already reigns in heaven. For the child of God there is a spiritual reality that transcends our earthly situation. What a comfort this is for us as we walk through the daily anxieties or perhaps the mundane and ordinary life.

No matter how worrisome or boring your current situation may be, there is a spiritual reality that you already reign with Christ and you will reign with Him for all eternity. God speaks of our future situation as our present situation as well. His Word is sure, and He will bring it to pass. We see some similar language in Romans 8 where Paul speaks of a domino effect of sorts of our salvation. Paul goes through a list of things that have happened before the world was formed such as the foreknowledge, predestination, and calling of God, then he speaks of the justification that has happened at the moment of salvation. But then he speaks of the glorification of the believer, and he says it in the past tense. We look around and realize that we certainly have not received those glorified bodies just yet, but in God's eyes it is as good as done. It is a spiritual reality though we do not fully partake in its benefits yet.

The result of this union with Christ is that for all of eternity we will stand as living illustrations of God's grace and kindness. We are the trophies of His grace. God puts the grace of Jesus on display through our lives.

The reality of our union with Christ changes our perspective. It comforts our hearts and it emboldens us to live for Him here on earth.

◆ ◆ ◆

How does an understanding that we have been united with Christ change the way that we live?

Read Romans 6:5-11. How should union with Christ impact the way we view our sin?

In what ways are we trophies of God's grace and a visual reminder of the power of the gospel?

SAVED by GRACE

WEEK TWO
♦ ♦ ♦
DAY FIVE

Ephesians 2:8-10

◆ ◆ ◆

Grace is the focus of these key verses and all of chapter 2 up to this point as well. It is only God's grace (*charis*) or unmerited favor that allows us to become children of God. Our condition was bleak as the start of Ephesians 2 has shown us, but His grace toward us is overwhelming. We are saved by His grace through faith, and there is *nothing* that we could have done to earn this salvation — it is a gift. The Greek grammar of this verse points us to the conclusion that the gift is not just one aspect of salvation but the entire package of grace through faith salvation. Stott paraphrases this way, "By God's grace you are people who have been saved through faith, and this whole event and experience is… God's free gift to you." There is nothing that we can do to earn this salvation. We cannot do enough good works to pay this price for ourselves. This passage is showing us the gospel, that we cannot do it on our own, so Jesus did it for us. He was crucified for us. He rose again for us. And now He extends this grace through faith salvation to all who will believe. Now that we have been saved by grace, Paul tells us that our faith should lead to good works. Tony Merida states that "works simply are not the root of our salvation. They are the fruit of salvation." We could do nothing to earn our salvation, but now we seek to live in grateful obedience for all that God has done for us. We are called God's workmanship. The Greek word is *poiema*, and it refers to a work of art or a masterpiece. *We are God's masterpiece.* His name is on us just as a master painter signs his name at the bottom of his painting. This world should look at us and know that we are His. We are not saved by works, but we have been created for them. We have been created for a purpose, and we see here that it is to do these preordained good works to bring God glory.

We are saved by grace through faith, and we live the Christian life by grace through faith. We need the gospel every day. Ezekiel 11:19-20 promised that this new covenant would be better than the old. We would be given in Christ new hearts and a new spirit so that we could serve Him. The new covenant is not just reformation — it is transformation. Ephesians 2:10 tells us that we have been created in Christ Jesus and that we are His workmanship. Ephesians 2:5-6 tells us that we have been raised with Him and made alive. This language serves to remind us that there was nothing we could do to earn this salvation. The dead cannot raise themselves. The work of art cannot paint itself. And the creation cannot create itself. It is all about His grace. It is all about Him. He has done for us what we could never do. This is amazing grace.

> "We are saved by grace through faith, and we live the Christian life by grace through faith."

We are God's workmanship, and this world should be able to look at us and know that we are His. List some things in your life that you want to be evidences to the world around you that you belong to God.

It is easy for us to be consumed with wanting to know God's will and purpose for our lives. These verses tell us what we have been created for! What do these verses tell us that we were made for?

Pause and thank God for the gift of salvation. Write out your prayer below. Pray that He would give you a renewed gratitude for salvation, and a desire to live out the calling to serve Him.

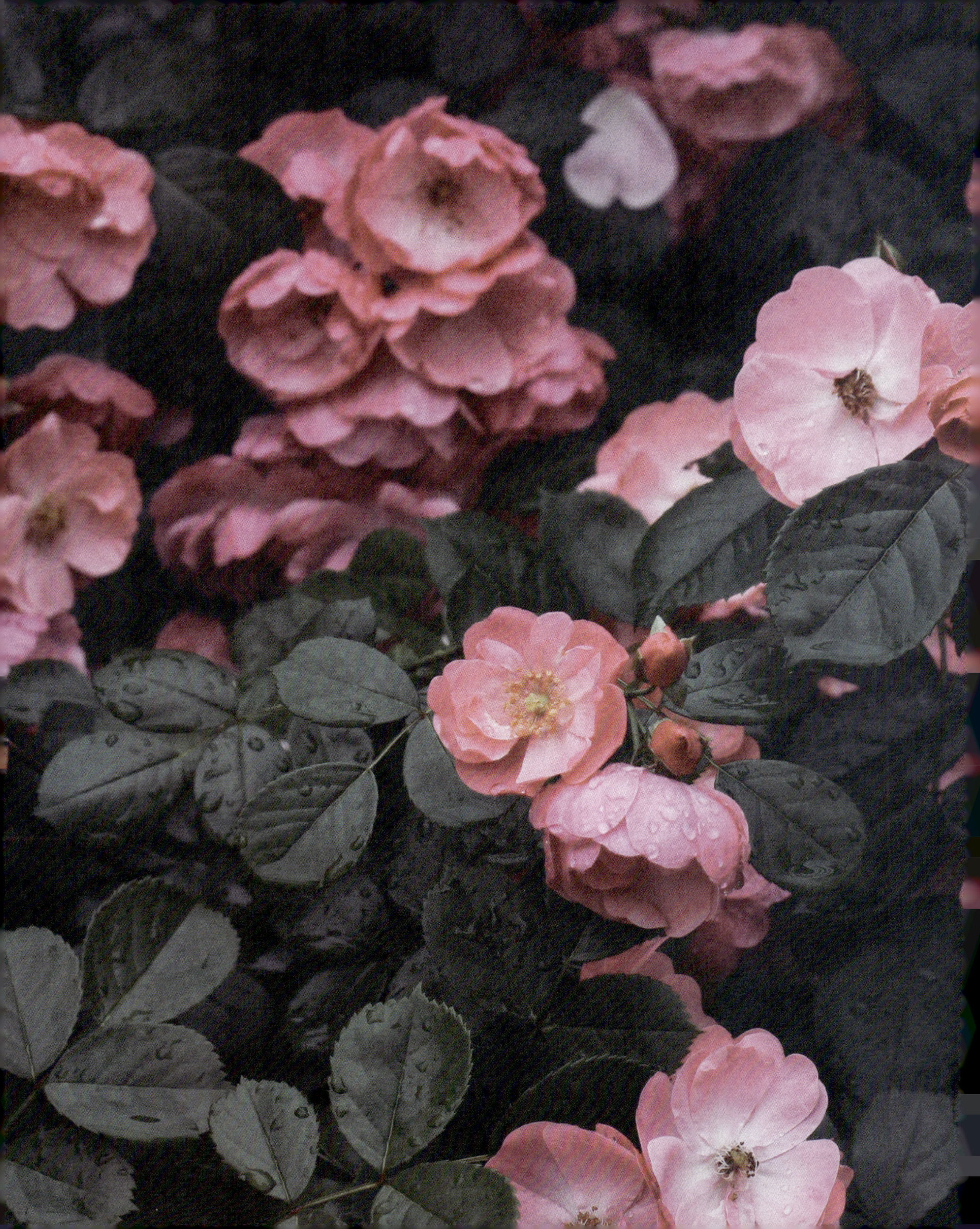

For you are saved
by grace through
faith, and this is
not from yourselves;
it is God's gift—
not from works,
so that no one
can boast.

◆ ◆ ◆

Ephesians 2:8-9

Cross references with unity language in Paul's letters

Unity language is constantly used by the Apostle Paul throughout the New Testament, and his letter to the Ephesians is no exception. The unity language that Paul uses in his letters emphasizes the sentiment that through the bond of Christ's blood, we are a supernatural family. We are united by the Gospel, we are built together into a household of God, we serve God's Kingdom together, and we bear the collective burdens of the body of Christ. Being bound together into heavenly siblingship allows us to accomplish things we may not have been able to do otherwise. We commit ourselves to the church because Scripture compels us to do so, and because our ministries are stronger and more impactful when we work together to reach the world and serve one another.

❖ ❖ ❖

UNITED BY THE GOSPEL

Ephesians 2:5, Ephesians 4:3, Ephesians 4:13, Colossians 2:2, Colossians 3:11, Galatians 3:28, 1 Peter 2:9-10, Romans 15:30

BUILT TOGETHER

Ephesians 4:16, Colossians 2:19, 1 Thessalonians 3:12, Galatians 3:28, 1 Peter 2:9-10, Galatians 6:10, 1 Corinthians 12:12-13, 2 Corinthians 13:11-12

SERVING TOGETHER

Ephesians 2:21-22, Ephesians 4:16, Ephesians 5:19-21, 1 Peter 3:8, 1 Peter 2:9-10, Romans 15:30, Galatians 6:10, 1 Corinthians 12:12-13

BEARING TOGETHER

Ephesians 2:21-22, Ephesians 4:2, Colossians 3:13-14, Colossians 4:2, 1 Thessalonians 3:12, 1 Peter 3:8, Romans 15:30, Galatians 6:1

WEEKLY REFLECTION

Read Ephesians 1:11-2:10

- Paraphrase the passage from this week.

- What did you observe from this week's text about God and His character?

- What does the passage teach about the condition of mankind and about yourself?

Week Two

- How does this passage point to the gospel?

- How should you respond to this passage? What is the personal application?

- What specific action steps can you take this week to apply the passage?

Brought NEAR

WEEK THREE

DAY ONE

Ephesians 2:11-13

◆ ◆ ◆

These three short verses show us who we are and what God has done for us. While the start of chapter 2 focused on who all people are before Christ, this section narrows its focus specifically to the Gentiles. For generations, Israel had been God's chosen people, but now the gospel was being spread to both Jew and Gentile.

Verses 11-12 almost list out bullet points of who the Gentiles were, and who every person is before they place their faith in Christ. We were Gentiles in the flesh, but also in our hearts. We were separated from God. We were alienated as strangers and foreigners. We were hopeless, and we were without God. The whole focus of the book of Ephesians is on being in Christ, but before salvation we were separated from Him. The Gentiles did not even know about the Lord. They did not know His covenants, or His promises of the Messiah, or the promise to bless all nations through Jesus. They were outsiders. We were once so far off from God. *Foreigners. Outsiders.* Verse 13 begins with a statement full and overflowing with hope. Just as verse 4 told us "but God" here we see "but now." We had a problem we could not fix, but God could. He kept promises that we didn't even know that He had made. He called us to be part of His chosen people. We were far off, but now in Him and through His blood we have been brought near. This is substitution (Isaiah 53:4-6). He took our sin so that we could be brought near (1 Peter 2:24). Like the Passover lamb, He paid our debt with His own blood (Exodus 12). He has redeemed us and made us His own.

He has done with His grace what we could never do. We are saved by His grace. These verses call us to remember all that we were and all that He is. We are now in Him, and we walk near Him. We were once far off, and now we are near. May we live each day near to His heart and praising Him for the grace that brought us near.

> "He called us to be part of His chosen people. We were far off, but now in Him and through His blood we have been brought near."

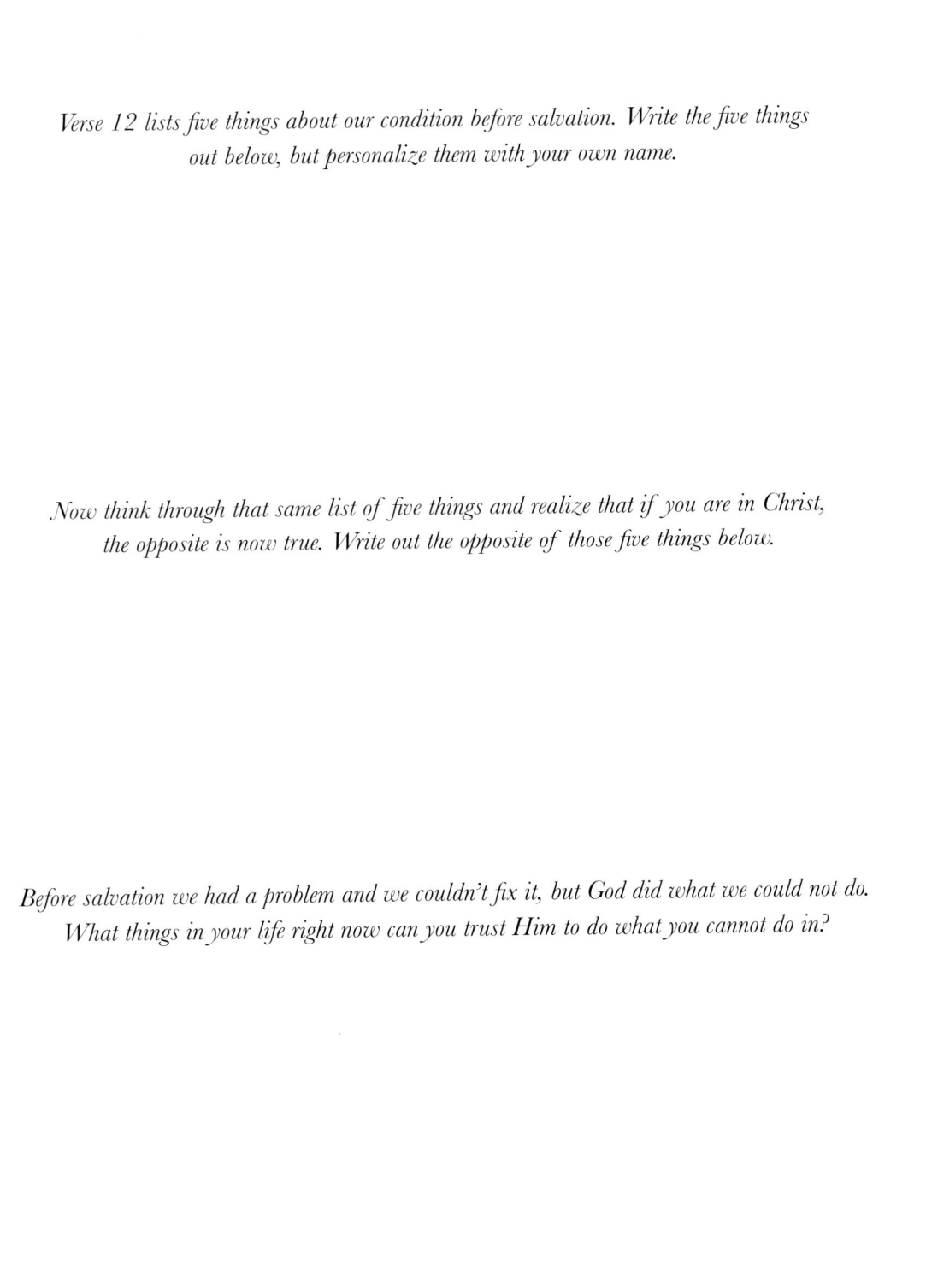

Verse 12 lists five things about our condition before salvation. Write the five things out below, but personalize them with your own name.

Now think through that same list of five things and realize that if you are in Christ, the opposite is now true. Write out the opposite of those five things below.

Before salvation we had a problem and we couldn't fix it, but God did what we could not do. What things in your life right now can you trust Him to do what you cannot do in?

HE IS
Our Peace

WEEK THREE
•••
DAY TWO

Ephesians 2:14-18

❖ ❖ ❖

He is our peace. *Jesus is our peace.* Scripture is full of this truth, from cover to cover, that Jesus is not just a source of peace or a peacemaker, but that He is our peace. Tony Merida says, "This was described in the Old Testament (e.g. Isa 9:6; Mic 5:5), affirmed in the Gospels (e.g. Luke 1:79, 2:14, 19:42; John 14:27), and explained in the epistles (Rom 5:1; Col 1:20; 3:15)." This peace is all-encompassing. It is security, safety, prosperity. It is the peace of salvation between God and man. It is the peace of Christ that transcends our circumstances, and it is the reason that Christians can live in peace no matter what suffering or situation comes their way.

Paul tells us that it is Jesus who has broken down the dividing wall between Jew and Gentile. At the time Paul wrote these words there was a literal wall in the temple that divided the court of the Gentiles from the rest of the temple where the Jews were. The wall would stand until the temple was destroyed in AD 70, but Jesus had already abolished it years before when He died on the cross. Through Jesus, a new people was made. In Jesus all races are united as one. All nations, tongues, and tribes are invited to come. Jesus preached peace to Jews and to Gentiles. He spoke in the temple, and He spoke to the Samaritan woman (John 4). Racial reconciliation is gospel-centered (Galatians 3:28, Colossians 3:11), and it is one of the ways that all things are being reconciled to Jesus (Ephesians 1:9-10). In His death, He abolished the law. This law of commandments refers to the ceremonial law, and it was abolished because Jesus fulfilled every type and picture that was pointing toward Him. Jesus broke down the wall between fellow men, and He broke down the wall between man and God. The veil of the temple that separated man from the holy of holies where God dwelt was torn in half from top to bottom when Jesus died on the cross (Matthew 27:51). That wall of separation was no longer needed because Jesus' sacrifice gave us access to God.

Now we can live in peace with each other and with the Lord because of what Jesus has accomplished. He has broken every barrier. He Himself is our peace.

> "Jesus broke down the wall between fellow men, and He broke down the wall between man and God."

How does the truth that Jesus is your peace impact the way that you live day to day?

Colossians 3:15 tells us to let the peace of God rule in our hearts. How do we practically do that? Read Colossians 3:12-17 to get some ideas.

Jesus has broken down every wall of division and calls His church to walk in unity and love to all people. How can you help break down dividing walls?

DWELLING
Near

WEEK THREE
✦ ✦ ✦
DAY THREE

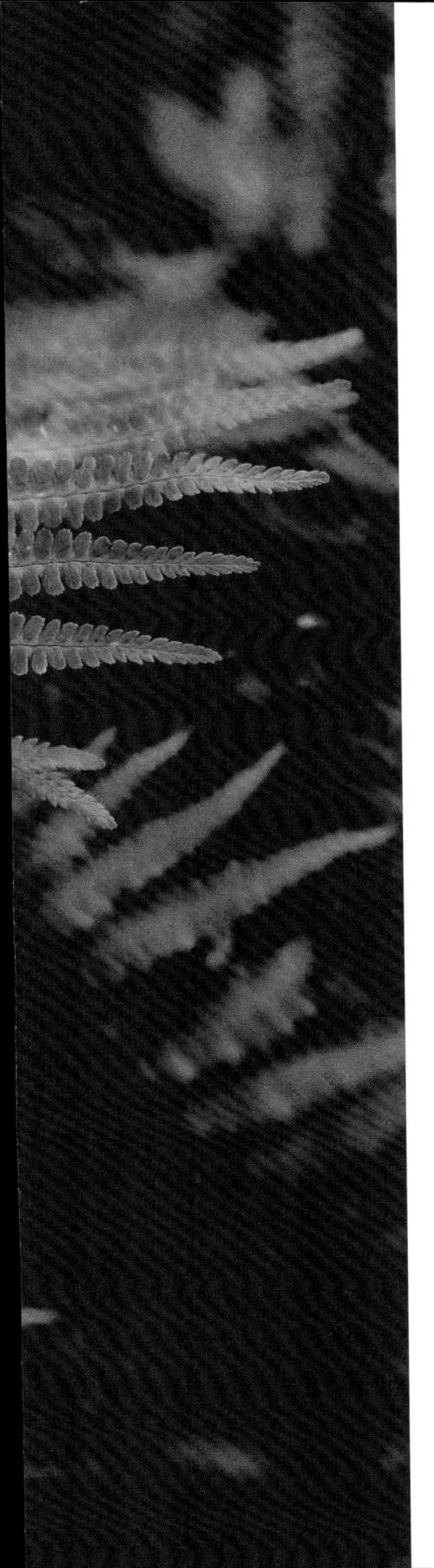

Ephesians 2:18-22

♦ ♦ ♦

All believers now are part of a new structure, and it is one that is designed to point toward our God. John Stott said of the church, "The church lies at the very center of the eternal purpose of God. It is not a divine afterthought. It is not an accident of history. On the contrary, the church is God's new community. For His purpose…is not just to save individuals and so perpetuate our loneliness, but rather to build up his church, that is to call out of the world a people for his own glory." Gentiles were once viewed as second class citizens, but Paul tells us that we are no longer strangers, aliens, or refugees. We have been given the full rights of citizenship. We belong in the kingdom. This is our place. These are our people. This "no longer" language reminds us of Galatians 4:7 where we see that we are no longer slaves, but sons and heirs. We have been adopted into a new family. Paul emphasizes that here in our passage as well by calling us members of the household of God. We have the full rights of citizens and also the full rights of sons.

The church is part of our identity, it is who we are, and we *need* each other. Paul now uses vivid imagery now of the church as the temple of the Lord and as His dwelling place, built on the foundation of the Word of God through the teaching of the apostles and prophets and Jesus Himself as our Cornerstone. *The church is built with a purpose.* From Eden to the tabernacle to the temple to Jesus, and now to us as believers, the collective church, God has had a dwelling place in each era of history. Ultimately, we will see this fully fulfilled in the new heavens when all is restored. We are His dwelling place. Jesus is not found in a particular building or physical location, but He is in His people. *He is with us.*

The church is now an important part of the life of the believer. We were not meant to walk this life of faith on our own, but in community. God has given us the church as a new family that will walk through this life with us and point us to the Lord. Tony Merida says, "It is a gift of grace to gather corporately and stir up one another to faith and good works (Heb 10:24-25). It is a gift of grace to love one another as Christ has loved us (John 13:34-35). It is a gift of grace to carry one another's burdens (Gal 6:2). It is a gift of grace to encourage one another and to be encouraged by one another (1 Thess 5:11). It is a gift of grace to be taught and admonished by one another (Col 3:16). It is a gift of grace to be allowed the privilege to give financially to further the gospel (2 Cor 8-9). It is a gift of grace to come to the table for communion (1 Cor 11:26)." We are created for each other. We are created to be His dwelling place. Both individually and collectively. He is with us — and that gives us strength to face this life.

> "We were not meant to walk this life of faith on our own, but in community."

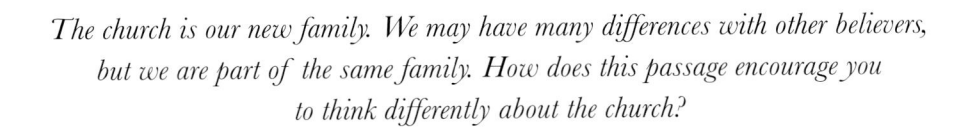

The church is our new family. We may have many differences with other believers, but we are part of the same family. How does this passage encourage you to think differently about the church?

Jesus is the cornerstone of the church. Read 1 Peter 2:1-10 and write down any ways this helps you understand Christ as our cornerstone and us as "living stones" being built together.

How has the church been a gift of grace in your life? How can you be that gift of grace for another believer?

WE ARE
The Church

WEEK THREE

♦ ♦ ♦

DAY FOUR

Ephesians 3:1-13

❖ ❖ ❖

Paul speaks to us of a great mystery. He comes to us as a prisoner for Christ. Though he was a prisoner of the government, he recognized that what had happened to him was not outside of God's divine plan for his life. So he comes with this great mystery. It does not mean a dark and eerie secret, but instead the idea of a divine truth that must be revealed by God. The mystery is the message of salvation through Jesus that is available to all, both Jew and Gentile. The message of Gentile inclusion was radical in Paul's day. Humanity is sadly prone to racism and the more subtle ethnocentrism that grieves the heart of our God who loves and celebrates diversity. So this message of Paul's was shocking. Paul is reminding them again that Jew and Gentile are now one. Jew and Gentile believers alike take part in every spiritual blessing through Christ (Ephesians 1:3) and experience the unsearchable and infinite riches of Christ (Romans 11:33). The gospel is truth and mystery and riches and blessing for God's people. It is *everything*.

So Paul comes with this truth and mystery of the ages. He presents to them the church as God's people called out from the world. He shows them a church called out by Jesus Himself who has made salvation possible. The message and the mystery is Christ and His church. It is through the church that the manifold wisdom of God is revealed. "Manifold" here means "many colored" and points us to the multicultural diversity of this church called out from every tribe, tongue, and nation. *Diversity is a gospel matter.* The multifaceted church is to point to the multifaceted wisdom of God. In our Savior, we can come boldly to our Father with confidence as His children, adopted as sons and heirs (Galatians 4:5-7). This is the priesthood of each believer. We no longer need a priest to intercede for us. We can come boldly to God Himself.

Paul's message was the gospel of Jesus and the centrality of the church in God's plan. The church is the vehicle for the spread of the gospel message. It is in community in which we are to grow in our faith and spiritual maturity, and it is God's plan for the ages. We are His *ekklesia* — His called out people for His purpose. Jesus loves the church and we should too.

> "It is in community in which we are to grow in our faith and spiritual maturity, and it is God's plan for the ages."

Paul wrote this letter as a prisoner, and yet he recognized that this was part of God's plan for his life. Paul wrote much of the New Testament from a prison cell. So much good came from his trials. What trials or difficult situations are you facing? Read Romans 8:28, and then write a prayer asking God to help you trust that He can bring good from your situation.

There is so much that we can learn from other members of the body of Christ. Getting to know people that are of different ages, backgrounds, races, cultures, social statuses, etc. can help us grow and see God's image in all kinds of people. How can you pursue diversity in your life?

Jesus loves the church and has called them to be the vehicle through which the gospel is spread and the way that His people grow. How can you love your church and serve God through it?

DWELL

WEEK THREE
♦ ♦ ♦
DAY FIVE

Ephesians 3:14-17a

❖ ❖ ❖

At the end of chapter 3, we find a transition passage. The first part of the book focused on who we are in Christ, and now we begin to transition into the second half that will tell us how we should live in Christ. Verse 14 begins with "For this reason." We find Paul in these verses overwhelmed and thankful for God's grace and character. These first three chapters have been showing us God's sovereign grace, and we find Paul praying with adoration for who God is.

Paul bows himself and kneels in prayer to show his great reverence for the Lord and his humility before Him. Kneeling was not something common in Jewish culture, but Paul was left so in awe of God that he knelt in worship. We are not commanded to kneel in prayer, but whether standing, sitting or kneeling, we should remember to bow our hearts before the Lord. Whether we are kneeling with our bodies or with our hearts, we should come to the Lord in prayer acknowledging that He is God and we are not. He has the power to help our situation and we do not. He has the power to change us and we do not. *Without Him, we can do nothing (John 15:5)*. Time in Scripture and prayer are meant to be done together. John Stott points out that truth when he says, "For it is in Scripture that God has disclosed his will, and it is in prayer that we ask him to do it." We see who God is through His Word, and then we ask in prayer for Him to transform us. Time in Scripture and time in prayer are meant to have lasting impact. They are meant to transform us from the inside out.

Paul begins a prayer for power and love in these powerful verses. We need God's power in us. We need to be transformed. This need for power and strength is highlighted by the use of the word "dwell" in verse 17. The Greek word here for "dwell" shows us that this is a permanent dwelling. Christ has dwelt in us through salvation, and now He settles in. D.A. Carson explains this as a couple who purchases a fixer upper and then seeks to spend their time making the home their own. He says, "When Christ by His Spirit takes up residence within us, he finds the moral equivalent of trash, black and silver wallpaper, and a leaking roof. He sets about turning this residence into a place appropriate for him, a home for which he is comfortable…when a person takes up a long term residence somewhere, their presence eventually characterizes the dwelling… when Christ first moves into our lives, he finds us in bad repair. It takes a great deal of power to change us; and that is why Paul prays for power…[He is] transforming us into a house that pervasively reflects his own character." God has made His dwelling place with us. He has come as our Immanuel and is God with us. And now by His great power, He transforms us into His image. We read His Word and we come to Him in prayer so that He can transform us with His almighty power.

◆ ◆ ◆

Chapter 3 begins with the words, "For this reason." As we transition into the second half of the book, we will begin studying how we should live based on who we are in Christ. Take a moment to look back over the first two chapters and write down what you have learned about who you are in Christ and what He has done for you.

Time in God's Word and time in prayer transform us into the image of Christ. How can you make God's Word and prayer a greater priority in your life?

God is at work transforming us by His strength. What area of your life does God want you to grow in right now? Write out a prayer asking Him to make you more like Him.

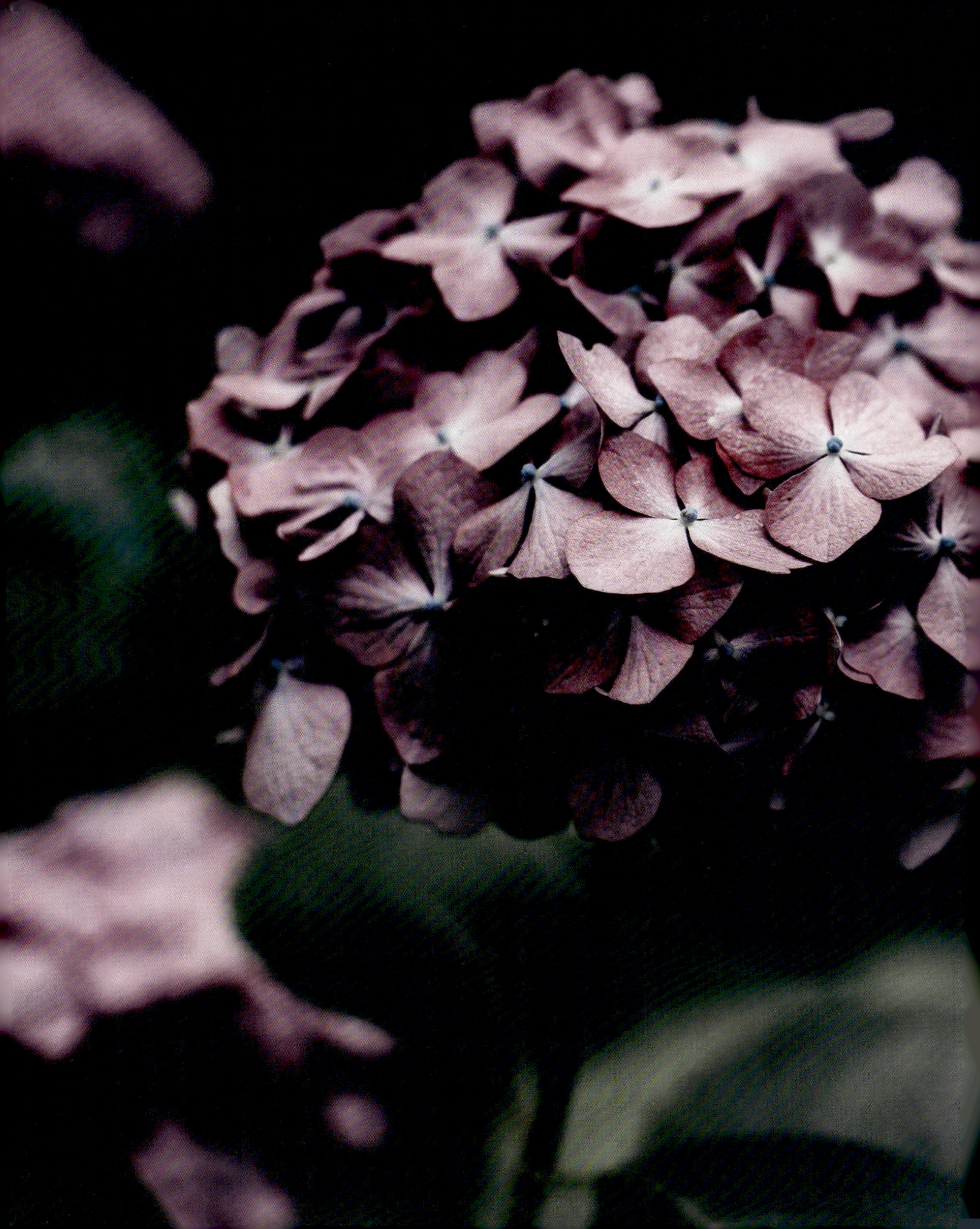

But now in Christ Jesus, you who were far away have been brought near by the blood of Christ.

❖ ❖ ❖

Ephesians 2:13

WEEKLY REFLECTION

Read Ephesians 2:11-3:17a

- Paraphrase the passage from this week.

- What did you observe from this week's text about God and His character?

- What does the passage teach about the condition of mankind and about yourself?

Week Three

- How does this passage point to the gospel?

- How should you respond to this passage? What is the personal application?

- What specific action steps can you take this week to apply the passage?

ROOTED AND
Grounded
IN LOVE

WEEK FOUR
♦ ♦ ♦
DAY ONE

Ephesians 3:17b-21

◆ ◆ ◆

In these verses, Paul continues this beautiful prayer. In the previous verses, he prayed for strength. Now he prays for love, but we must remember that we cannot understand His love without His strength. These concepts are so beautiful and so beyond our comprehension. The Christian life is a journey of constantly trying to know Him and His love more. Paul is not simply wanting us to have an intellectual knowledge of Christ's love, but to know it as a conviction of our souls because we have personally experienced it. My daughter Sophia passed away when I was 37 weeks pregnant. Before her passing, I would have told you that I knew God's love, but it was in the days and weeks after we lost her that I felt His love like never before. When I felt hopeless, He was my hope. When I was broken, He was my healer. When everything was falling apart, His love was steadfast and sure. Before, I knew God's love, but now I truly *know* it.

In these first three chapters of Ephesians we see the beauty of our God. Paul wants us to taste and savor the love he has described for us. Paul uses illustrations from nature and architecture to draw his point home.

He proclaims that we should be rooted in love. As a tree draws strength and nourishment from its roots, we draw from Christ and His love. We should also be grounded in love. He is our foundation, and our whole life and identity is built on His love for us. It almost seems like Paul cannot find the words to describe God's love as he speaks of the breadth, and length, and depth, and height. John Stott says, "The love of Christ is "broad" enough to encompass all mankind…, "long" enough to last for eternity, "deep" enough to reach the most degraded sinner, and "high enough to exalt him in heaven." As we strain our minds to begin to comprehend this incomprehensible love of God, we are left in adoration. We cannot be spiritually mature if we do not grasp His love. Again for Paul, his theology would lead him to doxology as he praises God for this amazing grace. Our God does immeasurably more than we could ever imagine, or dream, or ask, or think.

> "He is our foundation, and our whole life and identity is built on His love for us."

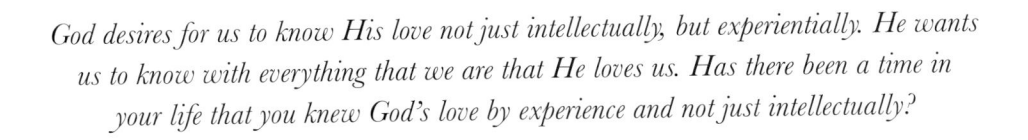

God desires for us to know His love not just intellectually, but experientially. He wants us to know with everything that we are that He loves us. Has there been a time in your life that you knew God's love by experience and not just intellectually?

We are to be rooted in His love. We are to be drawing strength from who He is just as a tree draws from its roots for nourishment, refreshment, and strength. How can you be rooted in Him and draw strength, nourishment, and refreshment from Him?

God's love is indescribable and beyond what we can even comprehend. Yet we can worship Him with our words. Write out a description of God's love and thank Him for who He is.

WALK *Worthy* OF YOUR *Calling*

WEEK FOUR

DAY TWO

Ephesians 4:1-3

❖ ❖ ❖

The first half of the book has given us a beautiful picture of the gospel, and now we will learn about the gospel-centered life. Paul is about to make our theology practical. He is urging us to make our daily lives match up with the theological truth that we know. To "walk" is referring to the way that we live our lives. We ask, "how should I live?" and Paul responds *"walk* worthy of your calling." These words pull us right back to chapter 1 where we saw that God has chosen and called us to be holy and glorify Him. Thayer's Greek Lexicon defines the word for "calling" as, "The divine invitation to embrace salvation in the kingdom of God." We have been invited into the story of redemption and given the privilege to build His kingdom here on earth. This is an invitation to live our faith and an exhortation to be like Jesus. Calling is not just something for pastors, and speakers, and missionaries, and writers — it is for every believer. *We have been called, and we have a calling.* We are called to live for Jesus right where He has placed us. Whether that is on a mission field, at a sink washing dishes, in an office, a classroom, or as a mother — God has called us to live in light of all that we learned in chapters 1-3. So often we struggle to be content with where God has placed us. We think that we could serve Him better if we had a different circumstance, but the circumstances of our lives are not an accident. We can live for Him, love Him, and serve Him right where we are.

Paul then begins to break it down for us and tell us exactly how we walk worthy of our calling. It all begins with humility. In a world that tries to boost our pride and says, "you are enough," we cling to the gospel that reminds us of our own weakness without Him, and proclaim that "Jesus is enough." Tim Keller says "The essence of gospel-humility is not thinking more of myself or thinking less of myself, it is thinking of myself less." When we see ourselves in light of the gospel, we are filled with humility and adoration to our God. Gentleness then is not weakness, but self-control. It is power under control. Next is patience. Is there anything more countercultural in our society than patience? But a lack of patience shows that we do not trust the Lord. So often we rush ahead because we think our way and our timing is better. Our refusal to be patient really shows our pride. We are then commanded to bear with one another in love. This is a call to tolerate each other. Doing life with people in community is not always easy, but we are called to unity. We are called to be eager for unity. God has given us unity in Himself, and now we are called to maintain it in the bond of peace. We are called to be like Jesus.

Our theology should change *everything*. What we believe about God should impact every aspect of our lives. Because He has called us in His grace, we now can seek to live in the grace that He has showered upon us. The gospel transforms us and then it compels us to live in light of that transformation. It calls us to not only experience grace, but to dwell in grace.

♦ ♦ ♦

In verse 1, we learned that our calling is to live a life that reflects the truth of the gospel that we learned in chapters 1-3. Where has God called you to be right now? How can you live out the gospel right where He has you?

We are called to be like Jesus. Verse 2-3 discuss several areas in which we can walk worthy of our calling. We should be seeking to cultivate humility, gentleness, patience, tolerance, and unity. Which of these areas is hardest for you right now and how can you grow in this area?

Our theology is what we believe about God, and it should impact every area of our lives. What are some practical ways that our theology should impact our daily living?

Grow IN CHRIST

WEEK FOUR
• • •
DAY THREE

Ephesians 4:4-16

♦ ♦ ♦

The beginning of this passage makes up what was likely a creed for the early church. We see the word "one" repeated 7 times as Paul focuses in on the importance of unity. These statements are foundational truths of the church. These are the declarations that many early Christians died for. The passage focuses on our one God in three different persons which gives us a beautiful glimpse of the trinity. Paul then begins to speak to the churches about spiritual gifts.

Spiritual gifts are mentioned several times in the Scriptures (Romans 12:4-8, 1 Corinthians 12-14, 1 Peter 4:8-11). Paul is not referring to the grace for salvation, but to the grace that He gives to each of His children in giving these spiritual gifts. God has graced us with spiritual gifts to serve Him and to build up the church. The church is a picture of unity through diversity. We are one body and we are one in Him, yet we have many diverse gifts as well as many cultures and nationalities. In Jesus, though we are different, we are *one* (Galatians 3:28). Each part of the body is needed for it to function as God intended. Every person and every gift is integral to the ministry of the church and the building of the kingdom. As believers, we have a holy calling and a divine purpose. And our God has given us everything we need to accomplish that purpose. This passage is almost like a domino effect of what Christ as done for us. He has given us spiritual gifts so that the church will be equipped for ministry, so that the body will be built up, so that there will be unity as we grow in our faith and knowledge of God, so that we will not be deceived by false teaching, so that we will be made mature in Him. It is a beautiful picture of God pouring out His grace on us to make disciples who make disciples. Truth and love are the foundation that make the whole process work. Truth and love are who our God is and should be the foundation for us as we grow in Christ and walk worthy of the calling that He has given us. May we lean into Him and His Word as we grow and mature in the love, truth, and grace that He has called us to walk in.

> "It is a beautiful picture of God pouring out His grace on us to make disciples who make disciples."

What gifts has God given you? How can you serve the church with them?

We are called to be disciples who make disciples. Who has poured into your life? Whose life can you pour into?

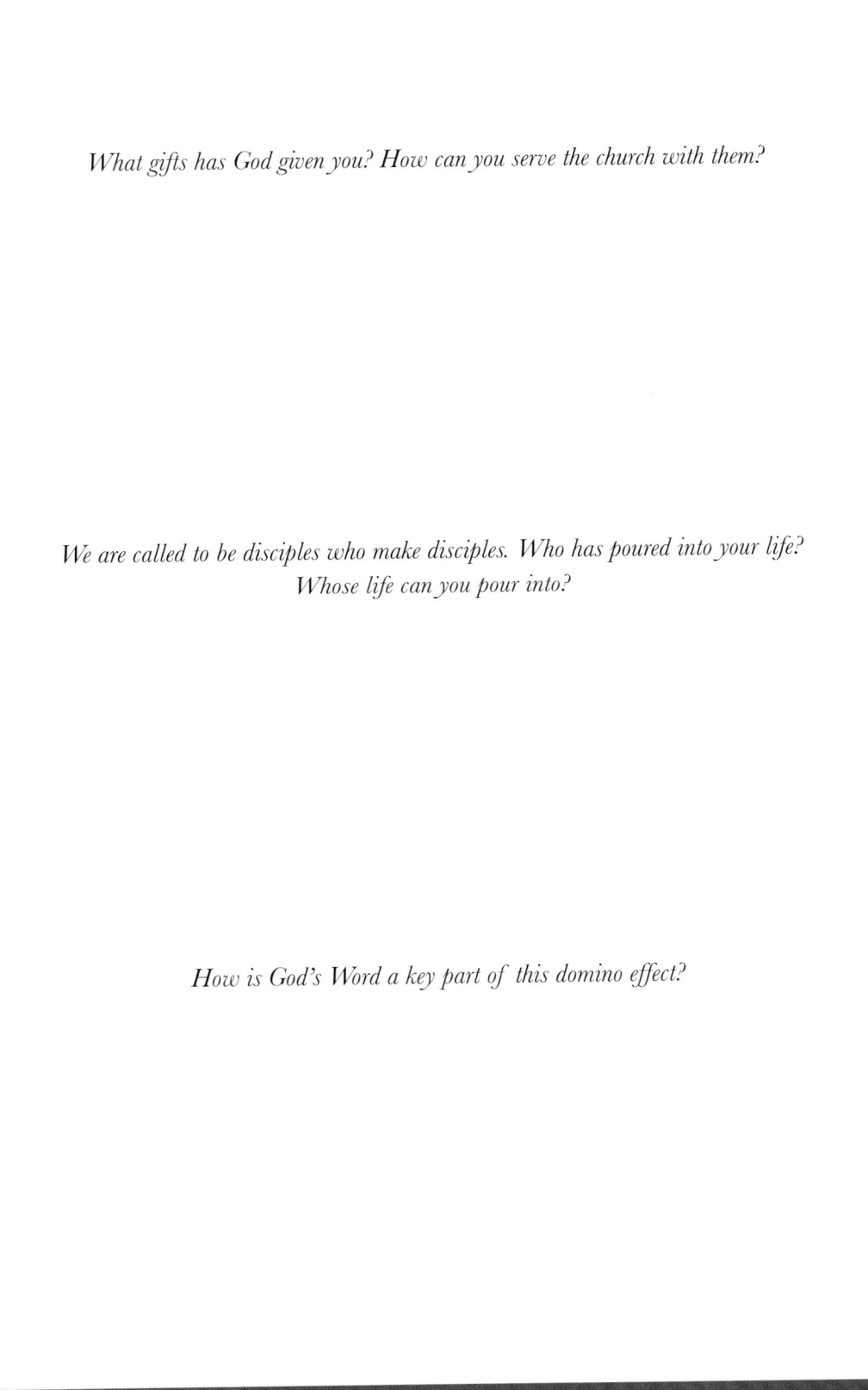

How is God's Word a key part of this domino effect?

A New IDENTITY

WEEK FOUR
•••
DAY FOUR

Ephesians 4:17-24

❖ ❖ ❖

We have been given a new identity. As believers, we are not what we once were. Paul reminds the church that they are no longer like they once were. The language reminds us of 1 Corinthians 6:9-11 when we see a list of unrighteous acts and then we see the phrase, "such were some of you." We have been saved from a life of sin, and we have been washed, sanctified, and justified. *We have been transformed from the inside out.* Now we are commanded to walk worthy of the calling that we have been called to. Paul tells us that this list is not how believers are supposed to live. A new creation should live in a new way. It is interesting to note that the word "about" is not present in the Greek verse 21. It could literally be read "you have heard him." As believers we hear from Him. It is not audible, but we hear Him speak through His Word and from His Spirit.

We have been made a new creation, and in salvation the old man is put off and we are recreated into a new man. We see this wording about "putting off" and "putting on" in other passages such as Colossians 3:9-10 and Romans 13:12, 14. This is something that happens at the moment of salvation in that we put on the new man, and also it is a daily process of us "renewing our minds" as in verse 23. This word for "renewing" shows a constant and ongoing action. We renew our minds through God's Word and through the Holy Spirit. This is a process of us setting our hearts and minds on the truth and allowing the truth to change us. In the Christian life, we must daily renew our minds, and we do this by dwelling on truth, thinking right thoughts (Philippians 4:8), and by learning who He is. We must think truth about who we are, our new identity in Him, and about who He is. As we do this, we give space for God to move and work in us through His Spirit and the Scriptures so that we can grow in holiness and in our new identity as a child of God. This world tells us a lot of lies, and the only way that we are going to combat them is by transforming our minds and thinking on the truth. We even tell ourselves lies, and we are going to have to take every thought captive to the truth (2 Corinthians 10:4-5). We are going to have to say *no* to the lies that the world tells and say *yes* to God's Word and surrender to the Spirit.

> "This world tells us a lot of lies, and the only way that we are going to combat them is by transforming our minds and thinking on the truth."

As believers, we have been given a new identity. What is your identity in Christ? Look back on the first half of our study for some clues.

We are called to put off our old self and put on our new identity. In one sense this happens at the moment of salvation, but it is also something that is an ongoing process as we become more like Christ. What is something that you need to put off? What is something that you need to put on?

We must constantly renew our minds and think on truth. What lies are you sometimes tempted to believe? Find specific passages of Scripture to remind yourself of that speak God's truth in those areas and write them below.

Called to
BE LIKE HIM

WEEK FOUR

♦ ♦ ♦

DAY FIVE

Ephesians 4:25-32

❖ ❖ ❖

We are called to be like Jesus – called to put off the characteristics of the world and to put on the characteristics of the Spirit. In this section, we see a focus on several aspects of what we should be putting on and off. All of the subjects listed in this section deal with relationships. Jesus does not only change the way that we interact with God and with ourselves, but also the way that we interact with other people. In essence, these verses are about holiness. Tony Merida points out that "Holiness is not just about saying no to sin; it is about saying yes to God." These verses exhort us to holiness, encourage us to say *yes* to God, and cause us to pray for Him to make us more like Himself.

We are urged to be people of truth and to flee from that which is false. Our God is truth, and we are called to live in that truth. We are called to not allow anger to cause us to sin. Anger has the potential for great harm. When left unresolved, it can cause us to become bitter, and Paul warns us that this unresolved anger can give an opportunity to the enemy. In the battle for holiness there is no place for us to give opportunity to our great enemy. We are also told to be honest in our work. We should work diligently as a testimony to our Savior and so that we can give freely. John Wesley said, "Work as hard as you can, make as much as you can, then give as much as you can." Paul then focuses on speech. He commands the church to not let corrupting, evil words come from their mouths. The Greek word here is *sapros,* and it literally means "rotting fruit." We must be careful to not speak rotting words. Words have great power. We can use them to harm or to heal. We can speak death, or we can speak life. We can speak refreshing, life-giving words, or we can speak rotting words that destroy. Immediately Paul warns against grieving the Holy Spirit. The Spirit is grieved when our actions do not honor the Lord. This should be a filter that we are constantly bringing our thoughts and actions before.

As Paul continues to list out the things that we should not do, we are reminded that as we walk with the Lord, we are constantly asking Him to take away our natural and fleshly inclinations and fill us with Himself. Bitterness and wrath, anger, clamor, slander, and malice are the things that we do naturally, but we are asking the Lord to transform us. Now because of what Jesus has done for us we can be kind to those that are not kind to us, we can be tenderhearted toward the unlovely, and we can forgive others and forgive ourselves because *we* have been forgiven. The word here for "kind" in Greek is *chrestos,* and even the word itself reminds us of Christ. It is His goodness and common grace, even to those who do not love Him back. Now we are called to love the way that He loved us. So we cry out to Him, *Lord make us like You.*

◆ ◆ ◆

This passage deals with our sanctification in relationships. Why can relationships be such a difficult area for us to be Christ-like in?

Look through the things covered in these verses and identify some that you need to grow in. Write them below and find some Scripture to encourage you in these areas.

Write out a prayer asking God to make you more like Him in those areas.

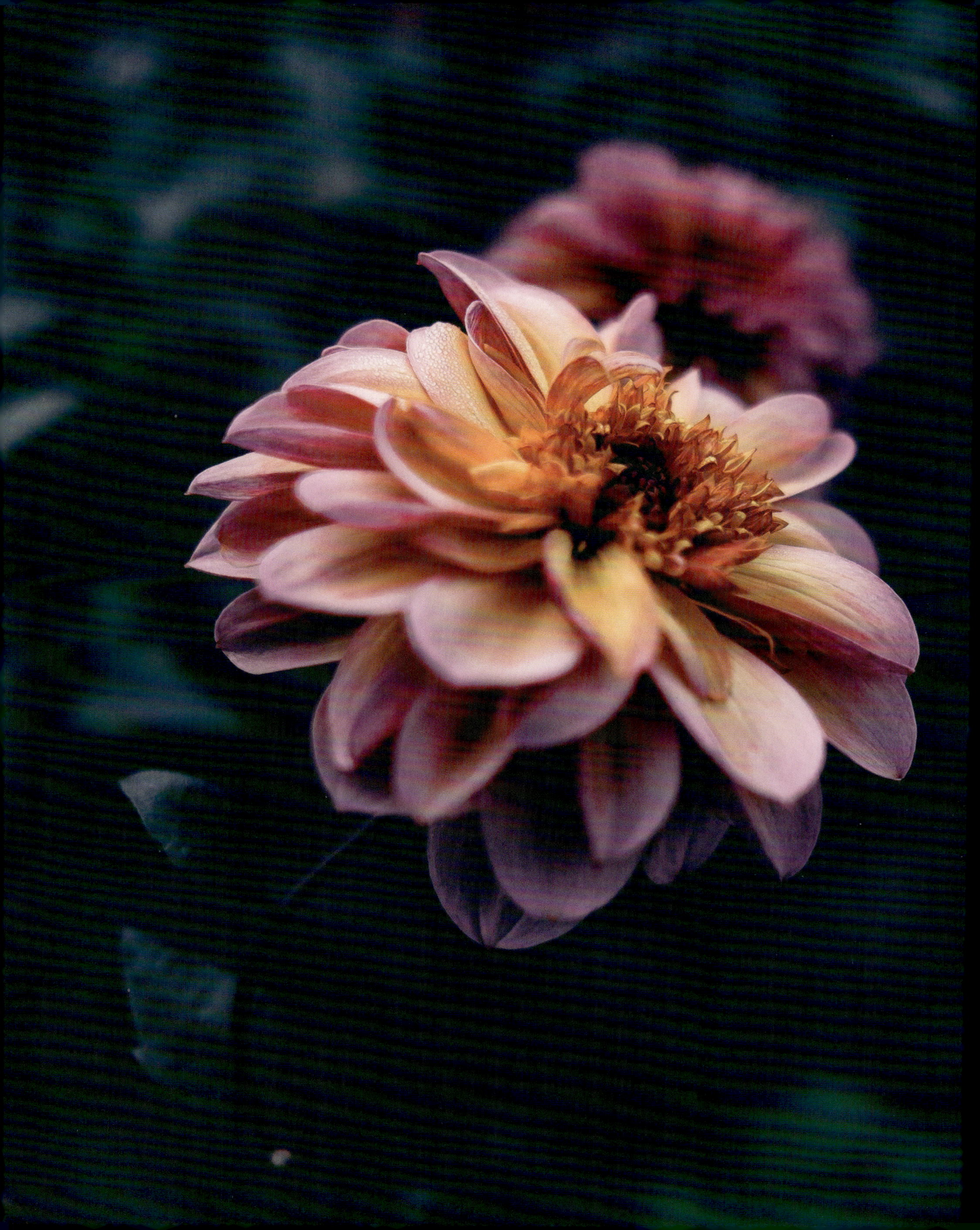

And be kind and compassionate to one another, forgiving one another, just as God also forgave you in Christ.

◆ ◆ ◆

Ephesians 4:32

WEEKLY REFLECTION

Read Ephesians 3:17b-4:32

- Paraphrase the passage from this week.

- What did you observe from this week's text about God and His character?

- What does the passage teach about the condition of mankind and about yourself?

Week Four

- How does this passage point to the gospel?

- How should you respond to this passage? What is the personal application?

- What specific action steps can you take this week to apply the passage?

Walk IN LOVE

WEEK FIVE
♦ ♦ ♦
DAY ONE

Ephesians 5:1-2

❖ ❖ ❖

Walk in love. Walk in light. Walk in wisdom. Ephesians 5 is going to tell us how we should walk, or live, as children of God. These verses seamlessly continue from the last section and call us to be imitators of God. Paul has vividly described who God is and what He has done, and now we are called to be like Him. We are called to imitate, or mimic, God. My daughter Stella likes to dress up as me. She will get my favorite heels, a cardigan from my closet, and a scarf or a necklace of mine and put it all on. She will think that she looks so much like me that she will try to trick my husband Jeremy into thinking that she is me. It always ends in lots of laughs and pictures sent to the grandparents. You see, children naturally want to be like their parents. They want to wear the same clothes and do the same things. God has called us as His beloved children to do the same. We are to imitate Him. To put on Christ. To do the things that He does, to wear the same character traits and to be just like Him. But if we are going to imitate Him and be like Him, we are going to need to know Him, and if we are going to know Him, we are going to need to know His Word. If we are going to be transformed into the image of Christ, we are going to need to know our Bibles.

We are then told to walk in love as Christ loved us. We are being commanded to do to others what God has done for us. We should love like He loves and forgive like He forgives, give like He gives, and show grace like He has shown grace to us. True love gives up ourselves and our desires for another person's sake. This isn't emotional "in love" kind of love — this is the kind of love that dies for another person. It is easy to say that we would be willing to die for our spouses or our children, but it is much harder to live out that same type of love day by day by selflessly putting their needs ahead of our own. 1 John 3:18 reminds us to not just love with words, but with truth and action. This sacrificial love is seen as an offering to the Lord. Like the Old Testament burnt offerings and the sacrifice of Christ were a sweet smelling aroma to God, so is our sacrificial love. May we love like He loved us and may we be more like Him. May we be transformed into His perfect image.

> "We should love like He loves and forgive like He forgives, give like He gives, and show grace like He has shown grace to us."

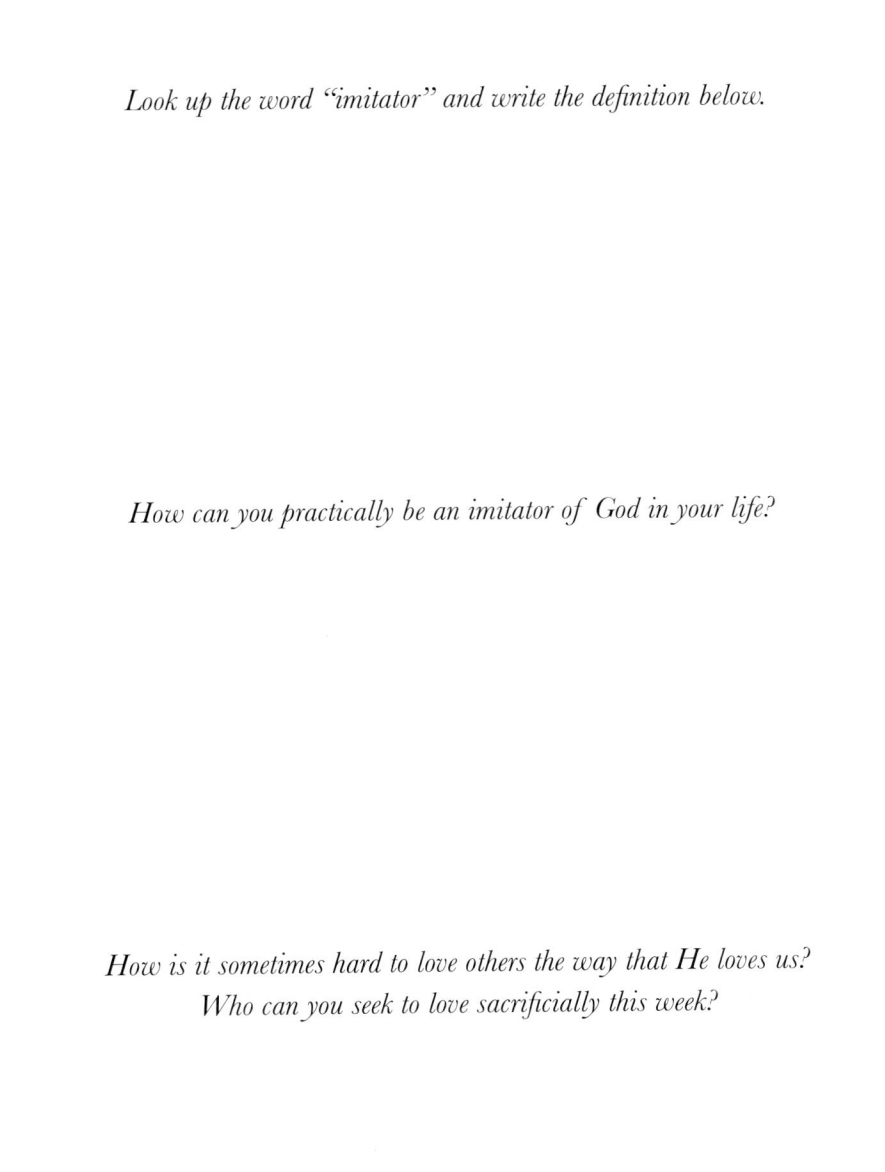

Look up the word "imitator" and write the definition below.

How can you practically be an imitator of God in your life?

*How is it sometimes hard to love others the way that He loves us?
Who can you seek to love sacrificially this week?*

WALK AS CHILDREN *of Light*

WEEK FIVE
♦♦♦
DAY TWO

Ephesians 5:2-14

♦ ♦ ♦

Paul begins this section with a warning to take no part in sin. He specifically addresses sexual immorality and covetousness. We must be careful not to focus too much on the outward problem that we neglect the root problem. Sexual sin of all kinds is so prevalent in our culture. Tony Merida reminds us that, "Your sexual sin problem is fundamentally a worship problem." This can be said of all sin. When we get our eyes off of Jesus, we are quick to begin worshipping other things, including our own sinful desires. We easily create idols of our hearts with things that we run to instead of to the Lord. We do not flee from sexual immorality because we think that sex is bad, but because we know that it is sacred and beautiful and very good in covenant marriage. Paul then speaks of covetousness, or greed. This wanting what others have, or wanting more, is the *opposite* of contentment. How easily we fall into this trap — whether money, food, sex, shopping, substances, or stuff. These things will never satisfy. The longing in our hearts is only filled by our God. The stuff of this world may satisfy for a moment, but our God satisfies for eternity.

Instead of being these things, we are told to

be thankful. Believers should not be known for their sin but for their supreme gratitude for God's goodness and grace. We are called to live a God-centered life instead of a self-centered life. When we realize what God has given to us, we don't have to look for more. Paul reminds the Ephesians that these sins have no value in God's kingdom. We are then urged to follow the Lord, to not be partners with sin, and to shine as lights. He has transformed us into light, and now He is calling us to be who we are in Him. We are to be light as He is light. As His light, we are to expose the darkness. We should be voices for justice in a world of sin. But light also opens the eyes of those in the dark and brings others to light. We do not partner with those in darkness, but instead we let His light shine through us and proclaim that our God satisfies more than anything this world has to offer.

The last verse is perhaps an early hymn, and it reminds us of what God has done for us. He has awakened us from the sleep of sin. He has raised us up from death. He has shone His light on us and now calls us to be His lights. We once were in darkness, but we have seen the Light — now we walk as children of the the One True Light.

> "We are called to live a God-centered life instead of a self-centered life."

All sin is a worship problem. People and things in our lives can easily become idols in our hearts. What things do you sometimes begin to "worship" in your own life?

How can you refocus your heart to the Lord when you catch yourself worshipping other things?

What does it mean to walk as children of light?

Walk in THE SPIRIT

WEEK FIVE
♦ ♦ ♦
DAY THREE

Ephesians 5:15-21

♦ ♦ ♦

How we live is important, and Paul now exhorts us to walk in wisdom and walk in the Spirit. We are to seek to live lives characterized by God's wisdom instead of the world's foolishness. And we can ask the Lord for this wisdom (James 1:5). We are called to prioritize our time and live for what truly matters. We want to be able to look back on our lives with no regrets because we gave our all to what mattered. We are to understand the will of the Lord. How often we get hung up and warned that we might miss our calling, but this verse is really just telling us to know our Bibles. God has shown us His will through His Word, so we should open our Bible each day looking to learn His will and His character. *He speaks to us through His Word, so if we want to hear Him speak, we need to open our Bibles.*

Verse 18 is the key verse of this passage, and the Spirit is key in our lives. We are commanded to not get drunk, but instead be filled with the Spirit. When a person is drunk, they are controlled or "under the influence" of alcohol. In contrast, the believer is to be controlled by, or under the influence of, the Spirit. We need the Spirit filling us, equipping us, controlling us, and influencing us instead of our passions or emotions. Our emotions are not always true, but God's Word is true. Paul will now go on to show us the results of living a Spirit-filled life, and in the coming verses we will see that we need the Spirit for all of our relationships. We see that Spirit-filled people are people of praise that sing of God's goodness to each other and to the Lord. Spirit-filled people are thankful people that give thanks in every circumstance (1 Thessalonians 5:18). They trust God in even their suffering and know that He is working in everything. We also see that Spirit-filled people have right relationships with each other as they submit to each other. The command to be filled with the Spirit is for all believers and it is an important one. The command is imperative *and* passive. In essence, we are commanded to let the Spirit fill us. Stott says, "We must never separate the Spirit and the Word. To obey the Word and to surrender to the Spirit are virtually identical." It is also important to note that this command is a present imperative. This is something that should be happening every day. We must be constantly yielding our hearts to the Lord and to His Word, and living filled with the Spirit. This should be the daily life of the believer. Coming before Him again and again, resting in His Word and being filled and renewed day by day because we need His power in us to face this life.

So we come before Him again with hands and hearts open, ready to be emptied of ourselves and filled with Him.

> "We must be constantly yielding our hearts to the Lord and to His Word, and living filled with the Spirit."

How are the wisdom of God and the wisdom of the world different?

As believers, it is easy to wonder about the will of God for our lives. But God has called us to lives of day by day and little by little obedience. He has called us to obey His Word. What are some things commanded in God's Word that you know that God wants you to do?

Being filled with the Spirit is an ongoing and daily part of the believer's life. What should it look like in your life to be filled with the Spirit?

SPIRIT-FILLED
Marriage

WEEK FIVE
•••
DAY FOUR

Ephesians 5:21-33

◆ ◆ ◆

We cannot overemphasize the need for being Spirit-filled in every aspect of life, and marriage is no different. As we read what Paul tells us about marriage, we must keep in mind that this is an extension of the call for all believers to be filled with the Spirit as well as the command for Christians to submit one to another. Verse 21 is a transition verse that bridges these sections, and in fact the Greek of verse 22 does not even include the verb "submit," but it is understood as being carried from verse 21. We could paraphrase it as, "believers are to submit to one another, likewise wives to their husbands." As we read about marriage, we must remember that marriage is a picture of Christ and the church. If we confuse this picture, we risk confusing the gospel to the world around us. We will learn that men and women are equal, but that they also have unique roles and needs. Women desire and need to be loved. Men desire and need to be respected. Paul is laying out a pattern for Biblical marriage, or how we can meet each others' needs. The commands to love and respect are about putting your spouse's needs before your own, and this act is a reflection of Christ and what He has done for us. *This isn't about yielding to cultural expectations but about reflecting the gospel.* When we live out this biblical pattern for marriage, we are putting the gospel on display for the world around us.

The beauty of the love stories of our marriages done God's way should point people to the immense love of our great God. God's plan is for the wife to demonstrate loving submission and for the husband to demonstrate loving service. The two concepts are very similar though played out by the unique, but equal, roles. The wife seeks to lovingly honor, and the husband seeks to be a loving servant leader. We can get scared of the word "submission," but as John Stott puts it, submission is "Love's response to love." As we love and honor each other the way that God has shown us love, we are demonstrating the gospel.

Again we must remind ourselves that the key to this hard-to-live-out goal is being Spirit-filled. It is the Spirit in us that enables us to be like Christ and lay down our selves for the good of the one we love in covenant relationship. And it is that Christ-likeness that displays the gospel to a watching world.

> "The beauty of the love stories of our marriages done God's way should point people to the immense love of our great God."

We are seeing that much of Paul's instruction stems back to that one command to live a life that is filled with the Spirit. How should being filled with the Spirit impact marriage?

In what ways does marriage point to the gospel?

Take the time to write out a prayer for your own marriage. If you are not married, pray for God to be glorified in your future marriage or the marriages of those around you.

FROM THE
Heart

WEEK FIVE
• • •
DAY FIVE

Ephesians 6:1-9

◆ ◆ ◆

Again we are reminded of the need for being Spirit-filled in all of our relationships. In this passage, we see that command played out for us in regards to parents and children and slaves and masters. Yet so many of the principles found in these verses can be applied to many different relationships and situations. In the first century, Christianity was very counter-cultural. Christians were known for doing things differently. In a world where women and children were seen as lesser, Christianity gave value to all life and pointed to the *imago dei*, or the image of God, in people of every age, gender, nationality, and social class.

Paul in these first verses speaks directly to children, reminding us that children are created in God's image and are an important part of the kingdom. Jesus had made this clear during His ministry, and Paul reinforced that truth (Mark 10:14). Paul emphasizes the importance of the obedience of children and also of the parent's role to point their children to the Lord. Children learn to obey God as they watch their parents obey God. The book of Ephesians has been telling us who we are and how we should live, and living this out is a demonstration and is instruction for our children. Dietrich Bonhoeffer said, "It is from God that parents receive their children, and it is to God that they in turn ought to lead them." Our job as parents is to encourage and not discourage (Colossians 3:2). Our job as parents is to point our children to the Lord.

Paul then moves to servants and masters. Again Paul is disrupting the cultural norms. It is important for us to note that Paul is not affirming slavery. It is also important to know that this slavery was much different than the racial and horrific slavery that is in America's past. This slavery was usually temporary, and often voluntary. It was used as a way for people to advance their social status. Even still, Paul does not affirm the practice. He calls both servants and masters to live differently. This teaching would undermine slavery and eventually help lead to abolition. The principles taught here are certainly applicable in our lives, our work, and in any area in which someone has authority over us or we have authority over another person. Everything we do should be for the Lord. There is no secular and sacred — it is all sacred because it is all for Him.

Paul focuses on the heart. So even if we are in a situation we don't love, or have a boss we don't love, we can work for the Lord. Tony Merida reminds us that Paul is teaching that they could "transfer masters, even if they could not transfer jobs." He goes on to say that the directions for employees are, "Work through Christ, like Christ, and for Christ." And to leaders "Lead through Christ, like Christ, and for Christ." No matter what we are doing, we should do it for Chris and for His glory (1 Corinthians 10:31, Colossians 3:17). No matter what we are doing, we are to be filled with the Spirit. Jesus changes relationships, and He changes *us*.

◆ ◆ ◆

How does being Spirit-filled impact relationships?

Our relationship with God is the perfect example of what a parent and child relationship should look like. How does God parent us? How should we respond to Him?

No matter what situation we are in, we can live for Christ and for His glory. What situation in your life is difficult or mundane? How can you purposefully live for the Lord in that situation?

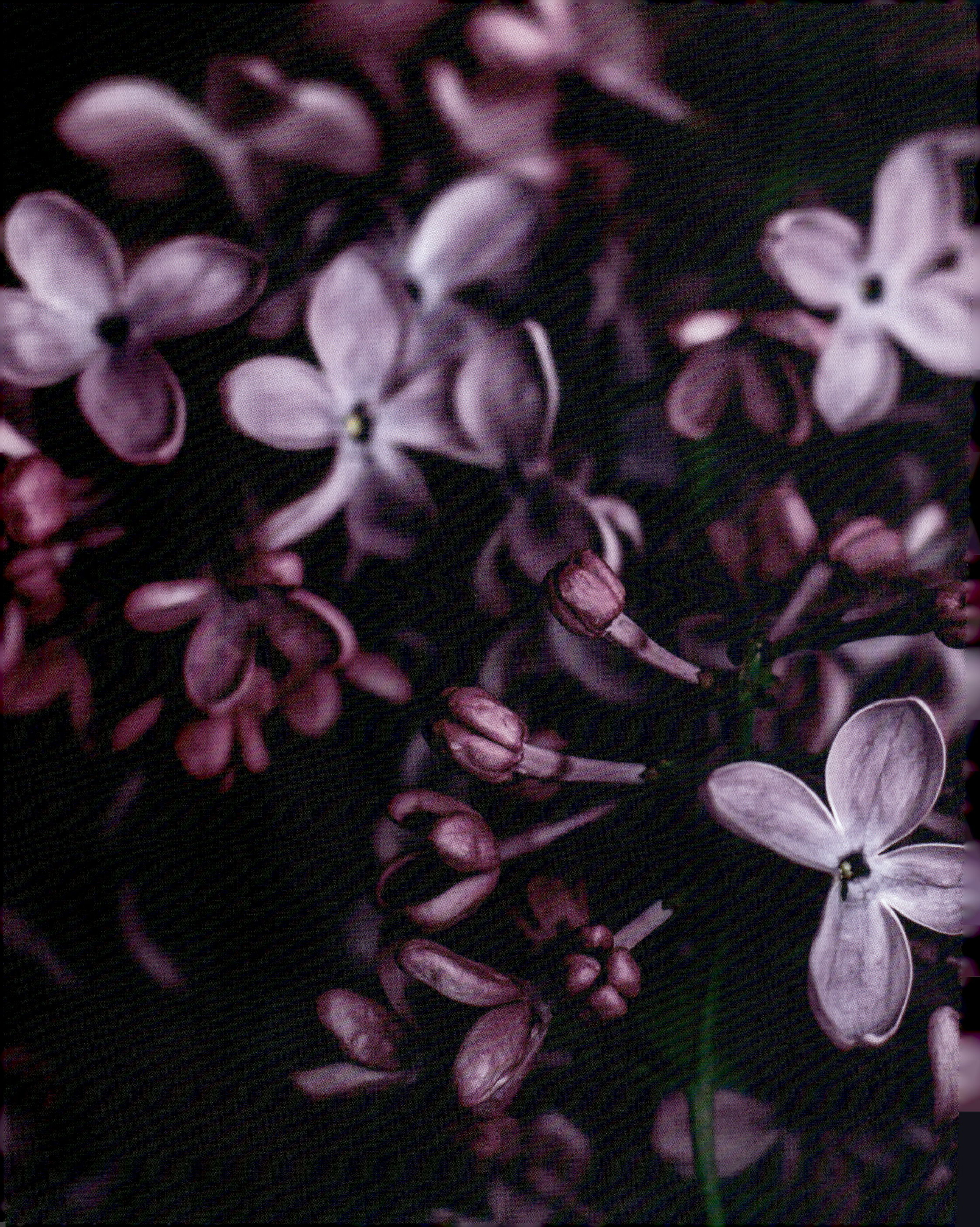

Therefore, be imitators of God, as dearly loved children, and walk in love, as Christ also loved us and gave himself for us, a sacrificial and fragrant offering to God.

Ephesians 5:1-2

WEEKLY REFLECTION

Read Ephesians 5:1-6:9

- Paraphrase the passage from this week.

- What did you observe from this week's text about God and His character?

- What does the passage teach about the condition of mankind and about yourself?

Week Five

- How does this passage point to the gospel?

- How should you respond to this passage? What is the personal application?

- What specific action steps can you take this week to apply the passage?

The Battle
IS THE LORD'S

WEEK SIX
♦ ♦ ♦
DAY ONE

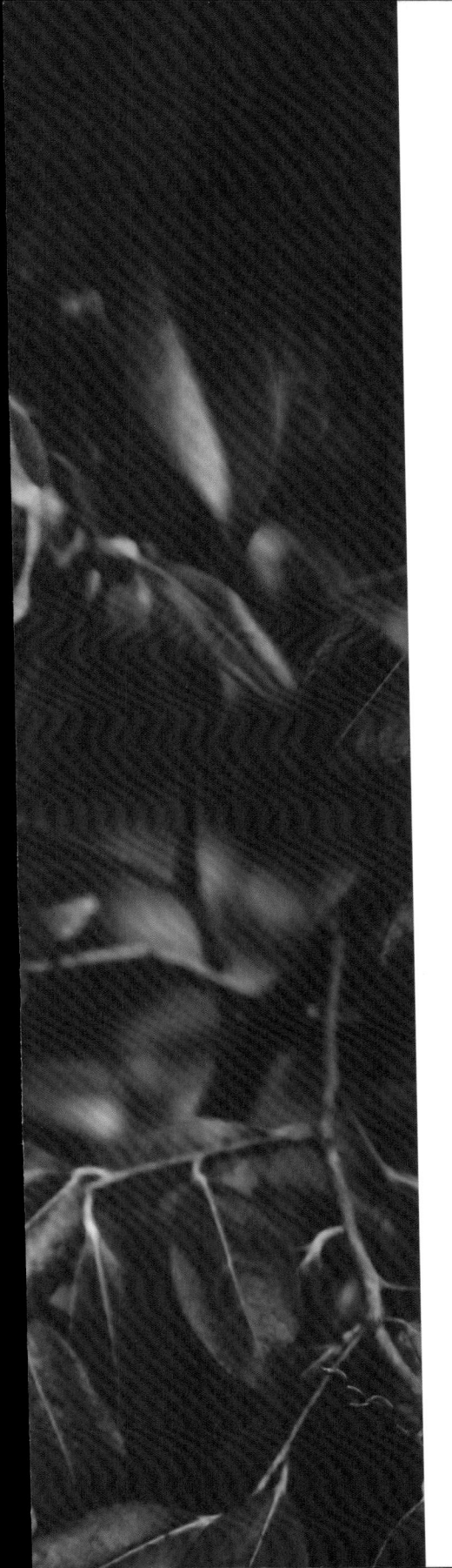

Ephesians 6:10-12

◆ ◆ ◆

We are nearing the end of our study of Ephesians. We have seen who we are in Christ and how we should live in this life, and now we are reminded that there is an unseen battle. Paul uses strong language and metaphor to get His point across. This is struggle, this is wrestling, this is battle, this is *war*. All throughout the Old Testament, we are told that God is a Warrior. He is our Warrior who is fighting for us and with us (Exodus 15:3, Zephaniah 3:17, Psalm 18:39, 35:1-3, 42:13, Isaiah 11:5, 49:2). Again we are reminded that as we face the battle of this life, we must be Spirit-filled. Learning about the armor of God is learning how to live the Spirit-filled life. So how do we fight this battle and stand for truth? Tony Merida says we must, "Be aware of the battle, be equipped with God's armor, and be devoted to prayer." If we are going to fight this battle, we are going to need to depend on the Lord.

Verse 10 calls us to be strengthened with "His" might. We need to be Spirit-filled and strengthened by God's power, because our own power will not do. We can't do this on our own. *We need God*. We are called to put on the armor of God because we have a very real enemy, and as Stott says, "Beneath the surface appearances an unseen battle is raging." We have a strategic enemy, and we must strategically defeat him. Verse 11 warns us of the schemes of the devil. He is cunning and crafty, and he attacks when we are distracted. He is studying us and looking for the areas we are weak in. He is looking for the areas that our family is weak in and the areas that our churches are weak in. He wants us to think that spiritual warfare is not a big deal. We must stand on guard. The word "wrestle" is used to describe this battle, and this reminds us that our enemy is not just in a conference room calling for missiles to be fired — this is hand-to-hand combat. Our enemy is up close and personal, attacking in strategic ways to the things we love most.

Paul clearly tells us that the battle is not against flesh and blood. We have a very real enemy, but our enemy is not people. So before you get angry at the difficult people and circumstances in your life, take thought that this may be spiritual warfare. We should show grace to people, but we must fight the enemy. Before you write this off thinking that the people in your life and your situation are so bad, remember that Paul was imprisoned, beaten, persecuted, and yet he was careful to recognize who his true enemy was. We must be careful to not give too much or not enough credit to our enemy. We must remember that we are in a very real battle, but we must also recognize that it is already won. This spiritual battle has already been won by Jesus. We are assured victory because Jesus has already defeated the enemy. We live in the already, but not yet. The cross has claimed victory over sin and death and our enemy, but now we wait for the day that we will see the full completion of that victory. So for now we fight as warriors in this spiritual battle, knowing that victory is sure and the battle is the Lord's.

◆ ◆ ◆

*Look up the cross-references about God being our warrior.
What do you learn about God from those verses?*

Why would Satan want us to think that spiritual warfare is not a big deal?

*So often we think that our people or circumstances are our enemy.
How can we keep our focus on our actual enemy?*

The Belt
OF TRUTH

WEEK SIX
♦ ♦ ♦
DAY TWO

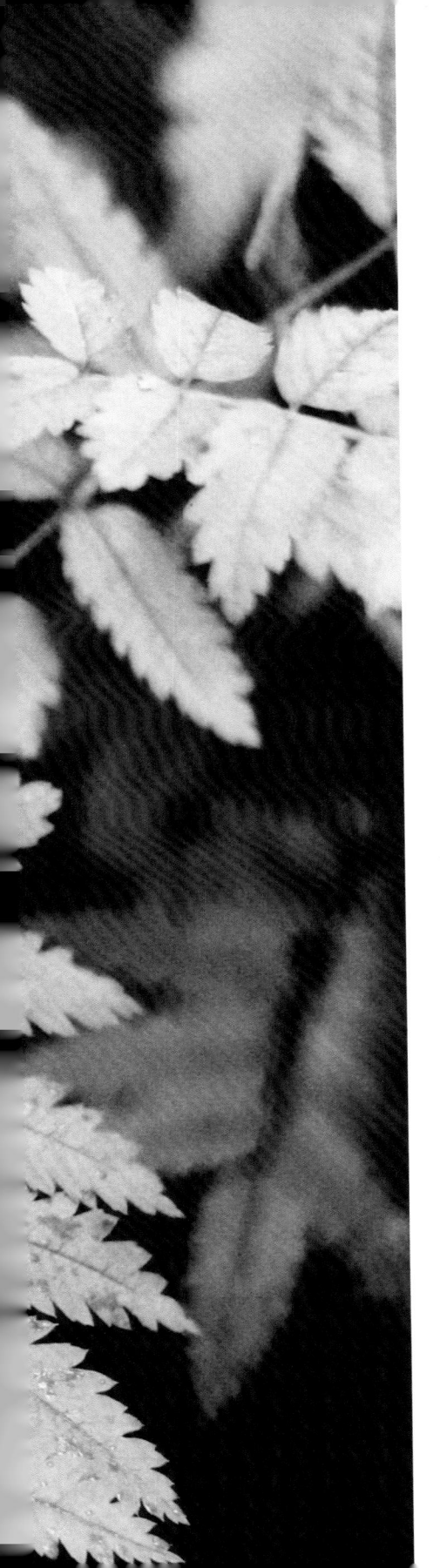

Ephesians 6:13-14

◆ ◆ ◆

We have been told who we are in Christ, and we have been made aware of the spiritual battle that is raging on. Now we are commanded to stand, and it is God's strength in us and this spiritual armor that make it possible for us to stand against the enemy's schemes. We must stand firm and resolved against the enemy with unwavering confidence in our great God. The first piece of the armor is the belt of truth that we are commanded to fasten on. We are commanded to fasten on the belt of truth or to gird up our loins. This doesn't happen by accident. We must consciously fasten on truth by getting into God's Word. Satan seeks to deceive us. We need to be aware that this is how he works. God's truth is the weapon that defeats the enemy's schemes of deception. We need to know how he works, but there is no reason to feel defeated. In fact, our knowledge of his tactics should give us the confidence that we need to fight back.

The enemy is going to try to convince us that we need the things that are the worst for us. He is going to tell us that what is bad is good and that what is good is bad. He will be subtle and tricky. He will play with our emotions and compel us to follow our hearts. He will try to convince us to follow our hearts instead of the truth of God's Word (Jeremiah 17:9). Our feelings do not always point us to truth, but God's Word is truth. We must stand firm in truth even when our emotions try to sway us. John Stott said, "Wobbly Christians who have no firm foothold in Christ are easy prey for the devil." We must consciously ground ourselves in truth so we are ready to stand up to the attacks of the enemy. Having on the belt of truth meant that you were prepared for battle, or whatever life would bring. It would help the soldier gather up the cumbersome robe and be able to move swiftly and effectively. God's truth does the same for us. It makes us able to face the situations of life and the schemes of our enemy.

We must preach the truth to ourselves so that we can combat the lies of the enemy. And if we are going to preach truth, we are going to have to know it. And if we are going to know it, we are going to have to know His Word.

What does it look like to stand against the enemy in your life?

"We must consciously ground ourselves in truth so we are ready to stand up to the attacks of the enemy."

How does the enemy subtly try to convince us that bad is good and good is bad?

What feelings do you sometimes think are true? What truth from God's Word can you combat those feelings with?

THE BREASTPLATE OF
Righteousness

WEEK SIX
♦ ♦ ♦
DAY THREE

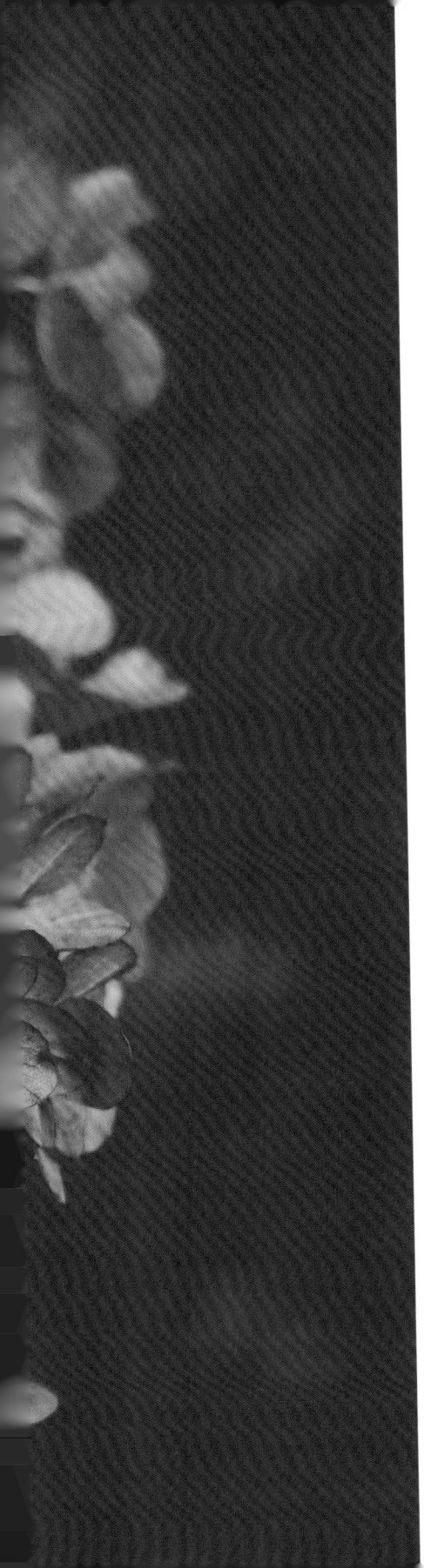

Ephesians 6:14

♦ ♦ ♦

Paul continues to explain to us the armor of God that we need to be putting on each day. We are to put on the breastplate of righteousness. The breastplate was meant to protect the most vital organs. The breastplate guarded the heart of the soldier in battle. In the same way righteousness is meant to protect our hearts. This righteousness is two-fold for the believer. Righteousness is not just "good works," because on our own we can do no good things. This righteousness is in one part the righteousness that comes only by the gospel in that Christ has taken our sin and in its place has lavished us in His own righteousness (2 Corinthians 5:21). This is the imputed righteousness that we receive at salvation. It is Christ's righteousness applied to us. In Christ, we have been made righteous, but He is also constantly making us righteous, or sanctifying us. So this breastplate of righteousness is both the imputed righteousness He has given to us and the practical righteousness that comes as we draw near to the Lord and live a life of holiness and righteousness.

Righteous living protects us like a breastplate. We are already declared righteous because we are in Christ, and now we must pursue righteousness. The breastplate of righteousness combines our total confidence in God, who has made us righteous through Jesus, and our continual desire for right living as an overflow of what God has done for us. Our enemy is smart, and he will try to go after our hearts. *We must fight him with righteous living.* We have already put on truth, and now we put on righteousness. Righteousness protects our heart, and then our heart pushes us to righteousness. However, when we live unrighteously, we open ourselves to the attack of the enemy. Righteousness protects our hearts like a breastplate. It pushes us closer to the Savior. God is the One that does this work of sanctification in us, and all that we must do is yield to His Spirit. May we yield to the Spirit, so that our hearts will be protected by righteousness.

> "Righteousness protects our heart, and then our heart pushes us to righteousness."

How does righteous living protect us like a breastplate?

As believers, we are declared righteous by God at conversion. We are also in a process of being sanctified. In what areas is God growing you in righteousness?

In what ways does unrighteous living open us up to the attacks of the enemy? How can you combat the attacks of Satan?

The Shoes
OF PEACE

WEEK SIX
• • •
DAY FOUR

Ephesians 6:15

❖ ❖ ❖

We have put on the belt of truth and the breastplate of righteousness, and now we are called to put on the shoes of the gospel of peace. These shoes Paul is referencing were the Caliga worn by Roman soldiers. They were gladiator sandals before they were in style. The sandals protected the feet of the soldier while also making him ready to face whatever terrain he would encounter. Paul tells us that we are made ready by the gospel of peace. We don't have to wonder what this peace is, because Paul has already told us in Ephesians 2:14 that Jesus Himself is our peace. The peace of Jesus lets us walk through whatever this life brings (Philippians 4:6-7). We can face life without fear because of His peace (Isaiah 41:10, 43:1, Psalm 55:22, 94:19, John 4:27, Philippians 4:6-7). The Caliga included spike-like cleats to help the soldier stand firm in any terrain, and that is what God's peace does for us.

The Greek word *eirene* used in this verse is the equivalent of the Hebrew *shalom*. Shalom in the Old Testament gives us a sense of wholeness and completeness. It conveys permanence. It speaks of peace in chaos. It is not just peace from war, but peace in the midst of the war of this life. The gospel is our permanent and enduring peace in a time of constant change and turmoil. It is Jesus who is our peace, and He is the One that this gospel proclaims. He takes our brokenness and our weakness and makes us whole and complete in Him (Colossians 2:10). The gospel is our firm foundation, and Jesus is our Rock. Have you ever seen a believer endure a trial and wonder how they made it through? This is how! Because of who He is, we can have peace in any circumstance or situation because we have Him. Our peace is no longer dependent on what other people think of us, our status or achievements, or our own effort — we have peace in Him. We have a firm foundation in Jesus Christ. *He is our Shalom.* Nothing can shake the permanent peace that we find in the permanent One (Isaiah 26:3-4). We find perfect peace in the Prince of Peace (Isaiah 9:6). *He is our Shalom.*

> "Our peace is no longer dependent on what other people think of us, our status or achievements, or our own effort — we have peace in Him."

Look up the cross-references listed about peace. Record any observations and how these verses help you understand the kind of peace that Jesus gives.

What things do we sometimes think peace is dependent on? How does the knowledge that He is our peace change our perspective?

What situation do you need Jesus to be your peace in right now? Write out a prayer asking Him to comfort you with His permanent peace.

The Shield
OF FAITH

WEEK SIX
♦ ♦ ♦
DAY FIVE

Ephesians 6:16

♦ ♦ ♦

The next piece of this holy armor is the shield of faith. We are told to put it on in every circumstance, and we are also told that it's purpose is to extinguish the flaming darts of the evil one. We have already learned that our enemy is scheming and strategic, and these flaming darts are just one more weapon in his arsenal. But we will not be defeated, and no weapon formed against us will succeed (Isaiah 54:17). God has given us ultimate victory in Jesus, and He gives us the tools for immediate victory. One tool against these flaming darts of our enemy is the shield of faith. The dictionary definition of faith is, "complete trust or confidence in someone or something." As believers, we put our complete trust and confidence in God who we know will be faithful. Faith is believing God at His Word. Faith is total confidence that God will come through for us. It is putting all of our eggs in one basket — because we trust Him that much. Faith is believing God no matter what darts the enemy may throw. Faith is confidence that God will do what He says He will do.

But this faith also leads to action. We trust His promises so deeply that we live and act as if it is already done. Faith is believing even when it doesn't make sense. The enemy will come with his fiery darts and accusation. He will try to convince us that his way is better than God's way just like he did with Eve in the garden. But this shield of faith is not just to protect us, but to extinguish those flaming darts that are being hurled at us like javelins. The fire of the enemy's lies goes out when it hits the shield of faith. His accusations cannot stand against faith in Jesus. They are instantly extinguished. The enemy will come at us with guilt and with scare tactics, and in faith we will believe that we are who God says that we are. He will come by trying to distract us or tempt us to sin, and in faith we will stand for truth and choose to obey God. Faith is confidence in the character of God, even when we don't understand His ways. We can place our faith in Him because He is faithful and He will be faithful to us (Hebrews 10:23, 11:1). We can trust Him. We can have full confidence in Him. We can trust that He is working even when we are not sure how. And that living and active faith will extinguish the attacks of our enemy.

> "Faith is confidence in the character of God, even when we don't understand His ways."

Faith is total confidence in God. What situation do you need to trust Him in right now?

How should your faith lead you to action?

How does faith extinguish the darts of the enemy?

Finally, be strong in the Lord and in the strength of his might. Put on the whole armor of God, that you may be able to stand against the schemes of the devil.

◆ ◆ ◆

Ephesians 6:10-11

Armor of God
INFOGRAPHIC

• • •

TRUTH
belt around waist
JOHN 14:6

RIGHTEOUSNESS
armor on chest
ROMANS 8:10

READINESS FOR THE GOSPEL OF PEACE
sandals on feet
MATTHEW 28:19-20

FAITH
shield that extinguished flaming arrows from the evil one
LUKE 17:5-6

SALVATION
helmet
1 PETER 1:9

WORD OF GOD
sword of the Spirit
HEBREWS 4:12

WEEKLY REFLECTION

Read Ephesians 6:10-6:16

- Paraphrase the passage from this week.

- What did you observe from this week's text about God and His character?

- What does the passage teach about the condition of mankind and about yourself?

Week Six

- How does this passage point to the gospel?

- How should you respond to this passage? What is the personal application?

- What specific action steps can you take this week to apply the passage?

The Helmet OF SALVATION

WEEK SEVEN
♦♦♦
DAY ONE

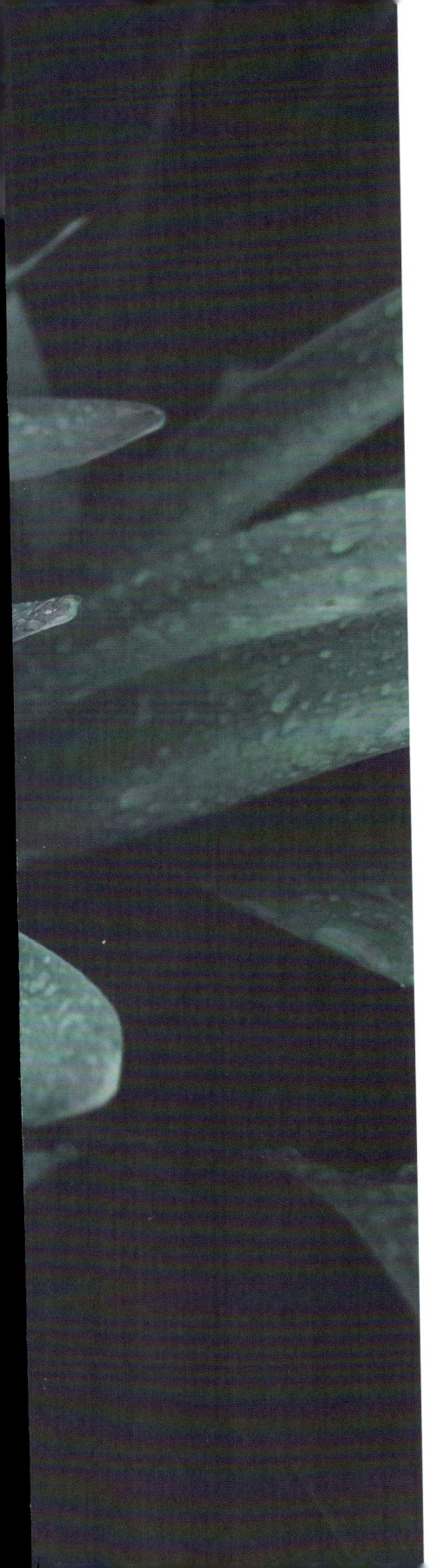

Ephesians 6:17

♦ ♦ ♦

The next piece of armor we must actively take up is the helmet of salvation, and this is all about our identity in Christ. This isn't about being saved again and again, but about reminding ourselves of who we are in Christ. Reminding ourselves of the gospel helps us to think correctly about who we are. It protects us from pride as we remember that we can do nothing without Him, and it shields us from insecurity and negative self talk as we cling to our position in Him. The enemy wants to get in our heads. Our minds are the biggest targets for his schemes, because he knows that if he can get in our heads, that the damage will trickle down to all aspects of our lives. 2 Corinthians 10:4-3 reminds us that we need to take captive our thoughts, and if we neglect to take captive our thoughts the enemy will use them as a way to attack our minds. Our thoughts are not always true. So we must consciously seek to align our thinking with God's Word. Remembering who we are in Christ will help us align our thoughts and minds to the truth of God's Word. In Him we are chosen, adopted, predestined, redeemed, sealed, saved, loved, brought near, etc. The book of Ephesians tells us all of these things about who we are, and now we need to live like it is true.

Ephesians 4:23 reminds us that we must seek to renew our minds and thoughts on the truth of God's Word. We must put on the helmet of salvation and be reminded of who we are. Salvation enables us to live victoriously. It is God's grace and power that have saved us, and now He also enables us to live this life victoriously. We do not need to be held captive by our thoughts — we need to take them captive. Our enemy will seek to strategically target our minds, so we must strategically fill our minds with God's Word. The truth of God's Word is our weapon against the enemy, because when we are reminded of who we are in Him, and we declare it and stand on God's Word, the enemy will flee. So we put on the helmet of salvation, and we live in the truth that we are His.

> "It is God's grace and power that have saved us, and now He also enables us to live this life victoriously."

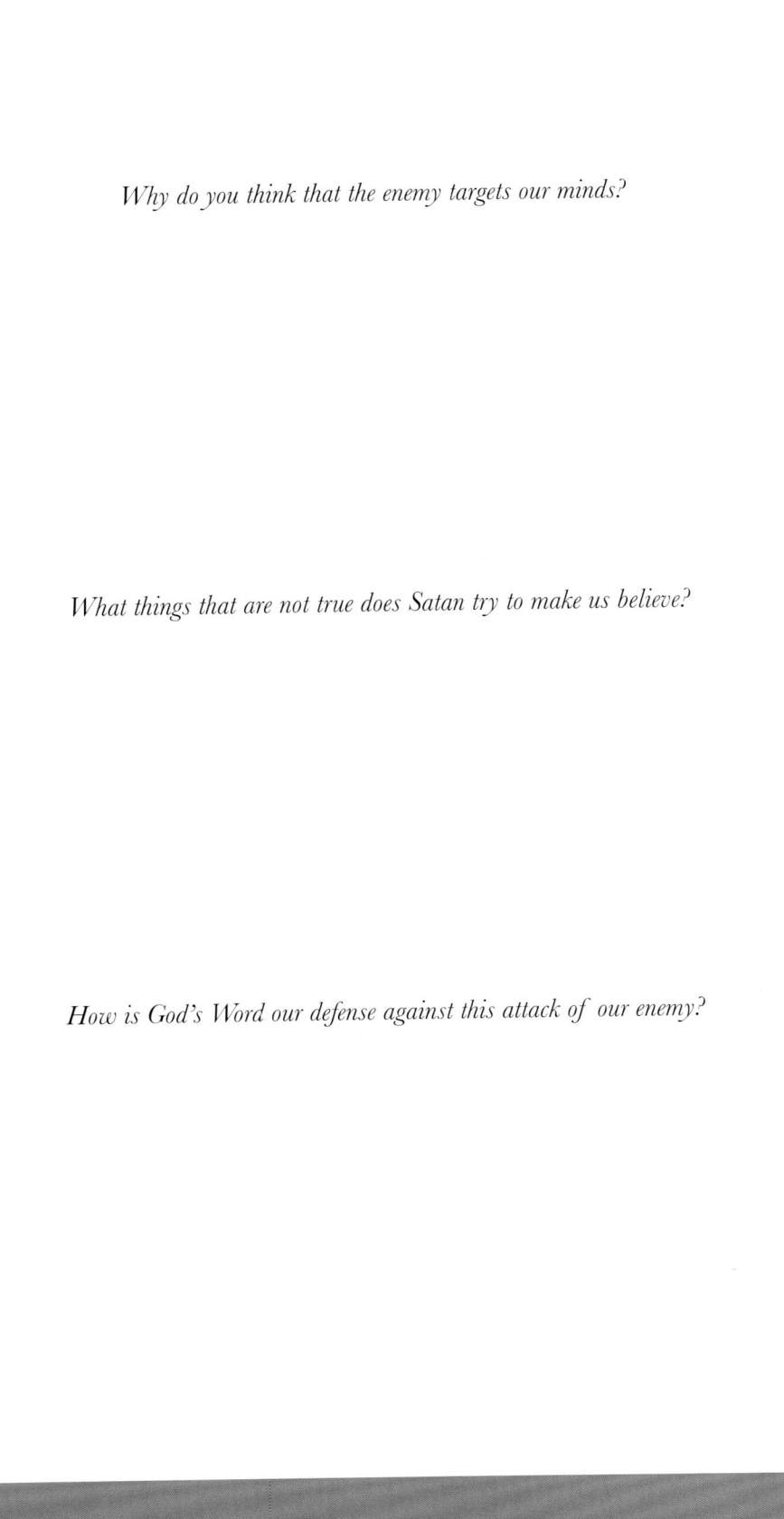

Why do you think that the enemy targets our minds?

What things that are not true does Satan try to make us believe?

How is God's Word our defense against this attack of our enemy?

The Sword
OF THE SPIRIT

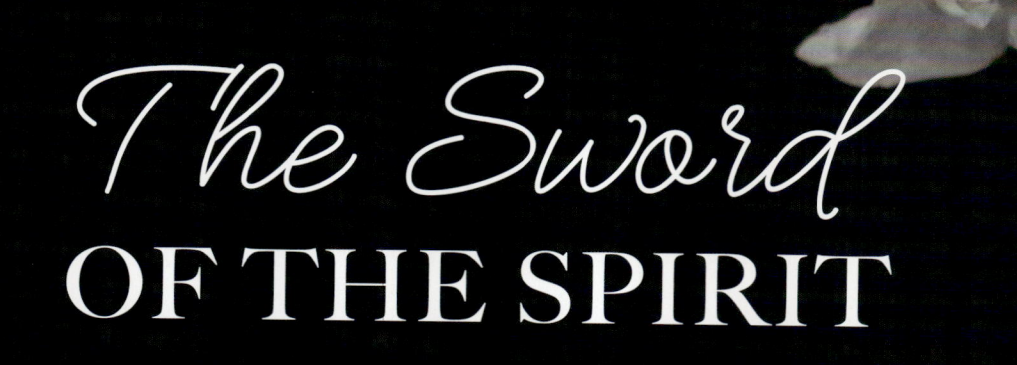

WEEK SEVEN
• • •
DAY TWO

Ephesians 6:17

♦ ♦ ♦

As we come to this final piece of armor, we see that it is a very important one. It is the only piece that Paul describes for us, and it is also the only offensive piece. God's Word is a weapon against the schemes of Satan. We have a very real enemy, but we also have a very real God. Our God has equipped us with His Word to defeat our enemy. The sword referenced here is a short dagger like sword. It is used for up close and personal, hand-to-hand combat. Our enemy is near, going after our hearts, our minds, our peace, our lives — and it is hand-to-hand combat with the Word of God that will defeat Him. Jesus is our great example, and we must remember that He used the Word of God to defeat the temptations of Satan (Matthew 4:1-11). If we are going to defeat the enemy, we are going to need to know His Word and use His Word.

God's Word is living and active (Hebrews 4:12). It has the power to defeat our enemy, and it has the power to convict our hearts. The Bible not only reveals our sin, but also declares our solution. Scripture has been breathed out by God and it is the thing that equips us for everything that we will face in this life (2 Timothy 3:16-17). God's Word is not only what equips us to defeat our enemy, but also what keeps us from sin (Psalm 119:11). It is God's Word that makes us strong and able to defeat the evil one (1 John 2:14). God's Word is our solid foundation. It is our comfort, our encouragement, and also our weapon.

This life is a battle, but our gracious God has given us everything that we need to have victory over our enemy. But we are going to have to have to open our Bibles. We are going to have to combat the lies of the enemy with the truth of God's Word. We are going to have to remember who we are in Him if we are going to defeat our enemy who is trying to lie to us and undermine Scripture. We are going to have to stand for the truth of Scripture, even when it goes against our culture. We are going to have to take the sword. We are going to have to know God's Word. We are going to have to study it. We are going to have to want it more than sleep, or food, or Netflix, or Instagram, or anything else. We are going to have to open our Bibles.

> "This life is a battle, but our gracious God has given us everything that we need to have victory over our enemy."

It is interesting to note that this final piece of armor is the only offensive piece. How does God's Word enable us to fight our enemy?

How does Satan attack you? What Scripture can you use to combat His attacks?

Write out some specific ways that you can make more time for God's Word so that you are more prepared to fight off the attacks of the enemy.

Praying at
ALL TIMES

WEEK SEVEN
✦ ✦ ✦
DAY THREE

Ephesians 6:18-20

♦ ♦ ♦

Though prayer is not assigned as a specific piece of armor, Paul doesn't even stop his sentence before calling us to pray. Paul is instructing us that as we take up each piece of armor, it must be done with prayer. We need spiritual weapons for this spiritual battle, and prayer is what gives these weapons power. We can't fight this battle on our own. We need the power of God to stand against our very real enemies, and our very real situations. So we call on Him in prayer because He is the one that has the power to defeat our every foe. Samuel Chadwick said "The great concern of Satan is to keep Christians from praying. He laughs at our toil, mocks our wisdom, but trembles when we pray." Prayer is very much a weapon against our scheming enemy. So we must find our strength in God, and call upon His name to go with us in this battle.

We stand through His power. We cling to the truth of His Word because He is in us. We live righteously as we abide in Him and Him in us. We have peace because it comes from Him and He goes with us. We take up faith, not just as a good luck charm, but with utter confidence in an unchanging and faithful God. We have security in our salvation and in who we are in Him because of who He is, and not anything that we have done. And we take His Word and we trust Him to illuminate it to us and help us to understand. We can't do it on our own. We need Him. And that is what prayer is for. We connect with Him and He walks with us through everything we face in this life. Paul's instructions are clear. We are to pray all times, with all prayer and supplication, with all perseverance, and for all believers. Prayer should not be our last resort, but our first defense. Prayer works not because of us, but because of Him. Paul is reminding us to stay awake and alert and to keep praying in this battle.

He also reminds us to pray for the spread of the gospel. He asked the Ephesians to pray for Him while he was in prison. He did not ask them to pray for him to be released, but for the gospel to go forth. We should be more concerned about the Kingdom of God than our own comfort. We must make prayer a priority, We must pour our hearts out before Him and watch Him work as we realize that He is our hope and our salvation.

> "Prayer should not be our last resort, but our first defense."

Though prayer isn't assigned a piece of armor, it is something that we are commanded to do through the entire battle. How does prayer impact all of the other pieces of armor in the battle?

Look back to the passage and circle or highlight the word "all" each time it appears. What does this tell you about the way that we should pray?

How are we sometimes tempted to use prayer as a last resort? How can we live with it as our first defense?

PEACE and GRACE

WEEK SEVEN
♦ ♦ ♦
DAY FOUR

Ephesians 6:21-24

♦ ♦ ♦

The book of Ephesians closes with Paul's heartfelt farewell and encouraging words. Paul speaks of Tychicus who would be the one to deliver this letter and encourage the hearts of those in the churches, and then Paul begins his final encouragement to those that would read these words. In many ways, he ends the book the same way that he started. He also touches on a few of the major themes covered in the book.

He speaks of peace, which is a theme throughout the book. We saw it in the opening greeting and then throughout the book with reminders that our peace is rooted in who Jesus is. This is the peace that only Jesus can give. It is a reminder that He Himself is our peace (Ephesians 2:5), and a reminder of the gospel of peace (Ephesians 6:15). He speaks of faith, and we are reminded that we are saved by grace through faith (Ephesians 2:8-9), and that we are to live by faith (Ephesians 6:16). He speaks of love, which Ephesians 1 so clearly demonstrated as we saw the vastness of the love of God for His chosen people. Then we were commanded to walk in love in the same way that Jesus loved us (Ephesians 5:2). And He speaks of grace, which is the way that we receive salvation (Ephesians 2:8-9), and the way that we live rooted and grounded in His love and grace.

Ephesians tell us who we are. It reminds us that we are His chosen people who have been lavished in grace and set apart for a purpose. And then it expounds on our daily living, walking, and abiding in God's grace. It reminds us to seek unity with God's people and to allow Christ to transform us. It reminds us to put on the armor of God so we can fight spiritual battles. It calls us to love our God with the same steadfast, incorruptible, and unfailing love that He loves us with. It calls us to live like Him and for Him. It reminds us of our identity that is not dependent on what we do, but on who He is.

May we live like Jesus and love like Jesus.

> "Ephesians tell us who we are. It reminds us that we are His chosen people who have been lavished in grace and set apart for a purpose."

The book of Ephesians tells us who we are and how we should live. What aspect of who you are in Christ stuck out to you? What aspect of how you should live stuck out to you?

What verse from Ephesians did God use in your life? Write it out below.

Write a prayer out thanking God for what He has done for you and asking Him to help you live for Him.

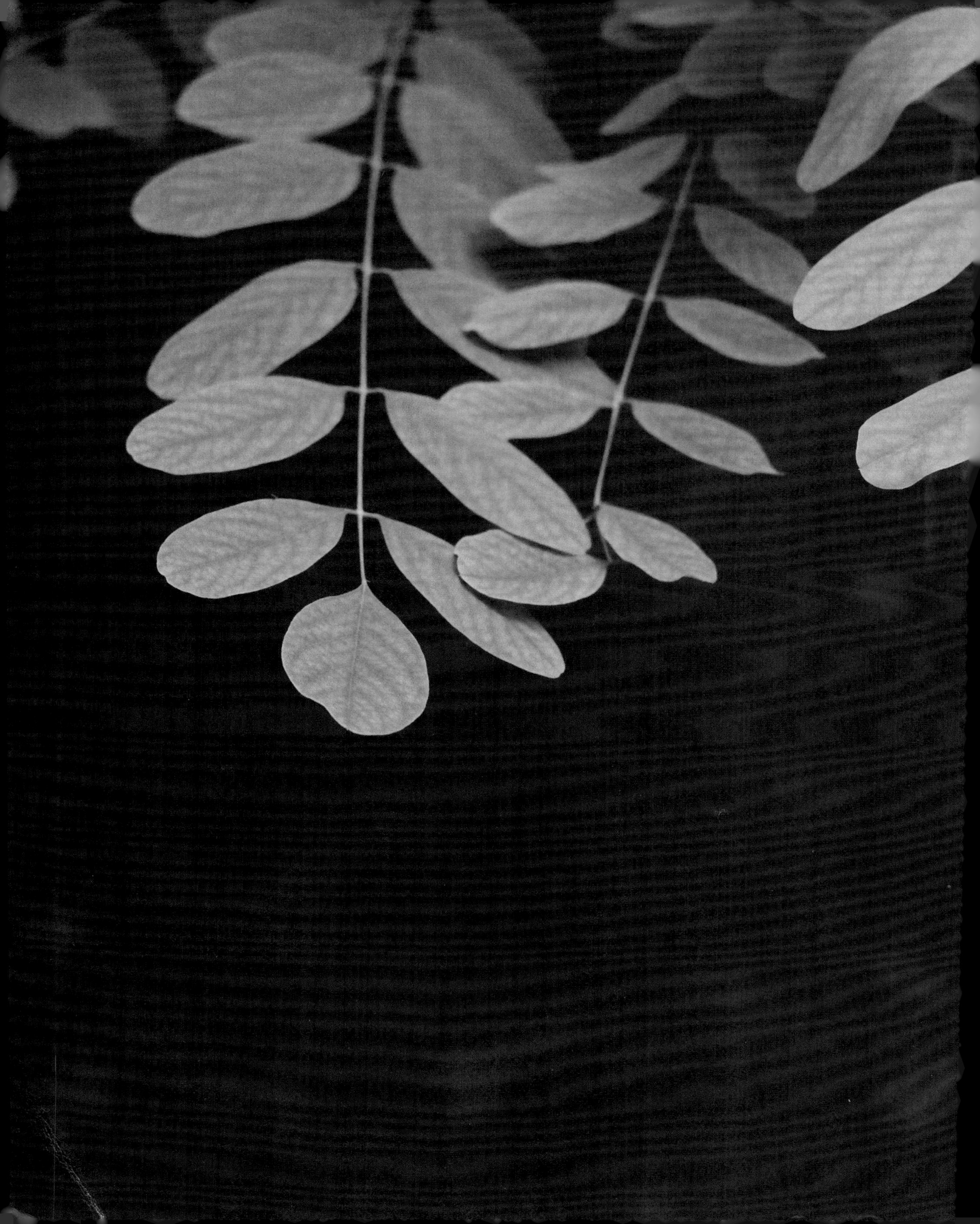

Peace be to the brothers, and love with faith, from God the Father and the Lord Jesus Christ. Grace be with all who love our Lord Jesus Christ with love incorruptible.

♦ ♦ ♦

Ephesians 6:23-24

Read Ephesians 6:17-6:24

- Paraphrase the passage from this week.

- What did you observe from this week's text about God and His character?

- What does the passage teach about the condition of mankind and about yourself?

Week Seven

- How does this passage point to the gospel?

- How should you respond to this passage? What is the personal application?

- What specific action steps can you take this week to apply the passage?

EPHESIANS
Reflection

WEEK SEVEN

❖❖❖

DAY SEVEN

Read the entire book of Ephesians

Take a day to read through the entire book of Ephesians again to see it as one cohesive letter.

What key words and phrases stick out to you?

What verse or passage has impacted you the most through the study of Ephesians?

What are the biggest lessons you have learned through Ephesians?

Write out a prayer as you reflect on the book of Ephesians.

What is the Gospel?

Thank you for reading and enjoying this study with us! We are abundantly grateful for the Word of God, the instruction we glean from it, and the ever-growing understanding about God's character from it. We're also thankful that Scripture continually points to one thing in innumerable ways: the gospel.

We remember our brokenness when we read about the fall of Adam and Eve in the garden of Eden (Genesis 3), when sin entered into a perfect world and maimed it. We remember the necessity that something innocent must die to pay for our sin when we read about the atoning sacrifices in the Old Testament. We read that we have all sinned and fallen short of the glory of God (Romans 3:23), and that the penalty for our brokenness, the wages of our sin, is death (Romans 6:23). We all are in need of grace, mercy, and most importantly—we all need a Savior.

We consider the goodness of God when we realize that He did not plan to leave us in this dire state. We see His promise to buy us back from the clutches of sin and death in Genesis 3:15. And we see that promise accomplished with Jesus Christ on the cross. Jesus Christ knew no sin yet became sin so that we might become righteous through His sacrifice (2 Corinthians 5:21). Jesus was tempted in every way that we are and lived sinlessly. He was reviled, yet still yielded Himself for our sake, that we may have life abundant in Him. Jesus lived the perfect life that we could not live and died the death that we deserved.

The gospel is profound yet simple. There are many mysteries in it that we can never exhaust this side of heaven, but there is still overwhelming weight to its implications in this life. The gospel is the telling of our sinfulness and God's goodness, and this gracious gift compels a response. We are saved by grace through faith (Ephesians 2:8-9), which means that we rest with faith in the grace that Jesus Christ displayed on the cross. We cannot save ourselves from our brokenness or do any amount of good works to merit God's favor, but we can have faith that what Jesus accomplished in His death, burial, and resurrection was more than enough for our salvation and our eternal delight. When we accept God, we are commanded to die to our self and our sinful desires and live a life worthy of the calling we have received (Ephesians 4:1). The gospel compels us to be sanctified, and in so doing, we are conformed to the likeness of Christ Himself.

This is hope. This is redemption. This is the gospel.